ADVICE

TERESA PESCE

Printed in the United States of America
First Printing 2022
First Edition 2022

10 9 8 7 6 5 4 3 2 1

To my beautiful Jimmy James, who makes me brave.

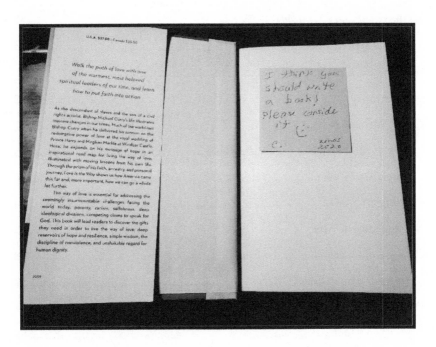

When my friend Cheryl gave me, "Love Is the Way"
by Bishop Michael Curry as a Christmas present,
she included this stickee note.
It was the seed that blossomed into the book you hold.

TABLE OF CONTENTS

AGING

We think aging is synonymous with getting old. Actually it isn't. Aging is just another word for living.

Are you alive? You're aging. When you were snugly bundled in the newborn section of the hospital, you were aging. Aging is a seamless continual process that begins at birth. We do it all our lives! It moves like a glacier—so slowly you can't see it, but inevitably.

Remember when aging was fun? First, we proudly added "and a half" to every year of our age. Then there was the rush of turning thirteen! Turning eighteen meant our first full-time job or our college years. Exciting! So, when did aging stop being fun? Perhaps when it became a negative.

One Frenchman lived his adult life in America but chose to live his final years in his native country. His reason? "In France, I am a man. In America, I am an old man." We are a youth-obsessed culture. Age-related cosmetic surgery is increasing among corporate males* for a reason called "survival." We are uncomfortable with aging. We fight it. We moisturize it, Botox® it, dye it, and gradually phase it out of our resume. We fear it. Some see it as an economic cloud on a horizon of uncertain distance; a slow subtractor of the senses, the mind, and the muscles that will ease us out of our home and into "a home."

The phrase "over the hill" originated in England in the 1900s and referred to turning forty years old because that age represented the middle of life. Today those black, "over the hill" birthday balloons are available for every decade after twenty! They jokingly remind us we are accelerating down the mountain of life right toward our funeral. The joke isn't funny, and it plays a trick on us that we miss. If the years of moving up the hill are aspirational, creative, and financially progressive, what is at the top? A pleasant plateau where we arrive, rule, and reign? Apparently not. There's just a black balloon announcing the beginning of the end.

"Over the hill" manages to completely ignore the value, worth, honor, and enjoyment of half of your life! And it is the half where you are knowledgeable, skilled, and mature enough to appreciate life as the young never can. It is the half where experience mellows to wisdom and the wanderings of lust become the home where love lives. It is the brightest half in so many ways, but we darken it with the lengthening shadow of a tombstone bearing our name with one date written and the other unnervingly blank.

Because the age process plateaus through our twenties, thirties, and even early forties, we identify ourselves by the body we have during those years. When the first evidences of aging come to our attention, the old-fashioned word "dismay" pretty well describes the average reaction: "consternation and distress, typically caused by something unexpected." *How could we not expect aging?* Well, we expected it, we just didn't know how we would experience it. I thought of each change as something to correct! The underarm area suddenly flabby? Lift weights! The first time it was difficult getting up from a deep knee bend to take something out of a low kitchen cupboard, I was astonished and added deep knee bends to my exercise routine.

Another reaction to the changes of my aging "suitcase" was humiliation at how matter-of-factly others took it! It was embarrassingly obvious that they saw me as older and fully expected me to wither away into a rocker. Case in point: as I was helping set up the stage and auditorium for a play, I chose not to carry heavy flats and furniture (in deference to my back, which had clearly informed me it didn't like lifting heavy things anymore) and started arranging the chairs. The director stopped me. "Don't do that," he said. "You'll do it for ten minutes and then have to sit down the rest of the day." I was shocked, insulted, and suddenly fearful that he was right! I meekly became a spectator to the setting-up process. Did I really look so insubstantial? I was only sixty-four! Astonishingly, because I didn't feel old inside, that age didn't seem "older" to me, as least not old enough to be infirm! But it did to a person in his forties.

Aging gradually goes from small moments of awareness to a morphing, multiplying "thing" that affects your entire body. There is a slight feeling that your body has betrayed you. It has moved your Dorian Grey* portrait from the attic and hung it in the living room.

I'd like to introduce you to the part of your being that is not aging. It's your soul, your spirit. It's the "you" that you carry around in your suitcase body. If you ask an older person how old they are inside, most of them come up with an age between twenty and forty. My internal age is about thirty-four years old. My external age is several decades older. And now I find myself doing this almost indescribable thing ... my true, internal self is accompanying my body into its older years. It's almost an alongside experience. I am being gentle with my body. Respectful of it. Appreciative of what it still can do. In the most curious way, I am accompanying myself on a journey. It's like having an "other awareness" of my own self. I didn't have this awareness when significant physical changes began.

I expected bifocals to adjust to close-up reading, but I pushed them back a few years with one contact lens focused for reading and another for distance. (Your eyes adjust.) It was nice to read restaurant menus without those tell-tale little half-glasses.

I expected silver hairs to lighten my natural blonde but didn't mind adding a bit of color back in because I knew hardly anyone who didn't enhance their hair.

Stairs surprised me. I began to notice that actors in movies would trot lightly up staircases, and sometimes sprint up two at a time. And I remembered when I could do that. My dad's offices were on the sixth floor at the university, and during my college years I would run up those six floors two steps at a time to visit him. I was only slightly out of breath at the top. I didn't expect to leap like an eighteen-year-old anymore, but it was surreal to notice I had to be careful to lift my feet on single stairs because I couldn't judge their height automatically anymore. After tripping once on stone stairs, I began keeping one hand unobtrusively near the handrail.

Memory deletions surprised me. I expected to begin temporarily forgetting names in light conversation because that is common and slightly amusing. But I didn't expect to forget details of office meetings. And I definitely didn't expect to forget we had met.

All these things seemed like insistent tugs on a youthful mask, revealing an aging human being. I couldn't plug every hole in my leaking memory. I couldn't feign eight-hour job energy. It was hard.

It all came to a point where I had to face this fact: I was no longer who I had been. At the time, that seemed like a bad thing.

It gradually dawned on me that aging is like an avalanche. It starts with pebbles and ends up with boulders. First you incrementally adapt with a small adjustment like being careful on stairs. Then one day you fully adapt with a change and move to a single-story home. And one day you ask yourself if you can still do the job you've done for decades. It feels as if you are under a hot spotlight and had better not make any more mistakes. It feels as if you should leave before someone has to ask you to. One day you release the guillotine blade on your own career. It is politely called retirement.

Taking that step felt as if I were stepping off a cliff into freefall that would end in death. It turned out to be the day I discovered I had wings! And it was the day I opened my own cage, so I was free to use them.

Remember "over the hill" meaning you were "past it"? That is wrong! "Over the hill" means you see a whole new vista! You shrug off the dragging weight of pulling your life up an incline and feel the exhilarating rush of acceleration as you coast with the wind in your hair like a kid on a bike.

I discovered our new single-story home was a pure delight! Everything I wanted was no longer upstairs when I was downstairs or vice versa. It was a lovely indulgence, so easy to navigate, and so quick to clean!

I realized retirement doesn't mean you stop working; it means you stop working for someone else.

My energy wasn't used up at work or dispersed in so many directions. I could devote it to interests and people I love.

Everything began to make sense. And it should have because what doesn't make sense is trying to live as if you are a different age and in a different time of life. You can't live where you were, for heaven's sake, you can only live where you are!

Now my time is mine. My freedom could never again fit into the cubicled confines of a full-time office job. Before, my workweek was entirely devoted to work because at the end of the day I was physically spent. Saturday was taken up with cleaning and chores. Sunday was my only day to relax. Everything I wanted to do was crammed into the meager time slots left over from my job. Now I can finish the chapter—finish the whole book if I like—because I can do chores any darn day I choose! I can run errands whenever I have my highest energy. Before, life was a corral with hay tossed in twice a month. Now I'm free to roam the mountains and valleys, and lounge in daydreams beside a lake.

It turns out "old age" was only "old age" when I tried to live the life of a thirty-year-old. I am the perfect age to live the life I get to live now! Actually I am always the perfect age with the perfect body to be who I am and do the work that I will be asked to do.

The world needs me as I am now. Let someone else lift the heavy stuff. Who cares? At any other time in my life, I could never have been who I am now, do what I do now, or help and serve as I can now. The self in this classic suitcase is quite happy!

My advice? Recognize that you are the age you are and live in the fullness of that. Recognize that you are ageless and live in the wonder of that. And if you'd like to discuss this further, I am available for coffee any time! (Don't be jealous!)

* "The Picture of Dorian Gray" is a Gothic and philosophical novel by Oscar Wilde in which Dorian Gray expresses the desire to sell his soul to ensure that his portrait, hidden in the attic, will age and he will remain young and beautiful.

** 'Boom in Cosmetic Surgery Linked to Age Discrimination', www.forbes.com, 2019.

** 'Fighting to Stay Competitive, More Men Turn to Surgery', www.cnbc.com, 2017.

ALL THE GOOD ONES ARE TAKEN

B elieving this sad cliché results in advising yourself, "Just give up. What's the point?" That is *terrible* advice to give yourself!

No, all the good ones are NOT taken! There's a reason why it appears that way, though, and here it is:

Men in love are quite different from men who are not in love.

(You doubt? Check out the lyrics to, "When A Man Loves a Woman.")

All the good men are not taken. They are temporarily disguised as men who aren't in love yet.

"All the good ones are taken" is usually said after a go-viral date disaster or the death rattle of an expiring relationship. Why are single men such commitment-averse, romance-resistant, communicationally constipated, selfish swine? Because …

The man who is not in love is logical and thinks with his brain. The man in love thinks with his heart and morphs into a "good man" because love is the great transformer.

It looks like this:

The same man who expects his dinner dates to meet him at the restaurant will change when he falls in love and become the man who thinks driving an hour out of his way to pick up his beloved at her home is simply the obvious thing to do. The guy who used to rant about Valentine's Day being a meaningless marketing ploy now browses jewelry stores looking for the perfect necklace featuring her birthstone.

Men don't realize how much they've changed when they fall in love, even though they may have to put up with a bit of verbal hazing from their friends who are secretly envious that they are not in love too. Men switch from logic to love without noticing. But to save yourself months and sometimes years of love limbo, you should know the differences between the two. Here are some behaviors to observe:

The airport is The Great Love Revealer. If he suggests you take a taxi to the airport, delete him from your contacts. If he drives you to the airport and drops you off, consider him a warm acquaintance. If he drives you to the airport and stays with you until you enter the restricted area, then finds a window and stands there watching until your plane is a speck in the sky, he loves you.

It's a logic vs. in-love thing. I knew a man who drove his girlfriend to the airport terminal, considerately made sure she had coffee and a good book, then was incredulous that she wanted him to sit with her until her flight was called. "Why?" he asked, irritable at her expectation that he should stay. "You're comfortable, you're all set, what good would it do if I sat here with you?" Not in love. When a man is in love, it simply doesn't occur to him to walk away and leave you sitting alone.

There are other Great Revealers.

Waiting

A man in love waits for you if you are held up at work or a rehearsal or at school or, in fact, anywhere at all. If he's not in love, it makes no sense to him that he should sit and wait for you until you're free, so he says quite logically to meet up with him when you're done.

Wedding Bell Clues

Wedding dates can give you clues about love as well. When a man is in love, a definite wedding date tends to be set promptly for as soon as possible. When he's not, the date is ballparked or avoided altogether because of the economy, the housing market, work commitments, former relationship wounds, parental pass-me-down marital hang-ups, the possibility that marriage would mess with relationship perfection, and the clueless question, "What's the rush?"

A man named Bill had a long term (and long-suffering) girlfriend named Kerry who found the wedding date to be a movable goal post. No matter where they decided to put it, it would skitter off and land two years away. I watched once when Bill was asked when he and Kerry were getting married. His pleasant smile froze in place, he lowered his voice, glanced around as if terrified someone would overhear, and muttered, "Two years!" He held up two fingers. "Two years," he repeated almost soothingly, trying to make himself relax. Those two years were far enough away to hold out hope to Kerry and make her stop asking about marriage, and far enough away to allow for a change of plans along the way. Then one day when Bill was traveling on business, he boarded an airport shuttle where he noticed a pretty woman take a cigarette from her purse. He took a lighter from his pocket. They married two weeks later.

The crash of Kerry's heart reverberated through all their friends. To be happy for him and sorry for her was socially excruciating for everyone. Kerry moved on and moved away.

Don't suffer like Kerry. Know what love looks like.

Jack Fulton had a girlfriend named Mandy who loved him dearly. She adapted to the unpredictability of his footloose, adventurous life. (One day she came home and deduced that Jack was back from traveling because she found an iguana in her bathtub!) And then the day came when marriage-proof Jack met the elegant and exotic widow of a political leader, fell in love with her, and married her. Mandy, who for years had accepted all Jack's reasons and rationalizations against marrying, discovered he had nothing against marriage at all. He just didn't want to marry her.

Don't be like Mandy. Unless you like iguanas.

In fairness to Bill and Jack, they genuinely thought they didn't want to marry anyone until they met a woman they *did* want to marry. I think that is because our language has only one word for love. It needs one more:

The Fifth Element: Marriage Love

We say we love our parents, pizza, and poodles, not to mention our friends, films, and fiction. The same word describes very different kinds of love. The Greek language offers four words to more precisely describe love: agape (unconditional, like God's love), familial (family love), philia (friendship love, as in Philadelphia, the City of Brotherly Love), and eros (romantic love).

I am going to add a fifth descriptor: marriage love. When you're in marriage love, you want to marry the one you love. It's just that simple.

The difficulties come when the one who *isn't* in marriage love doesn't want to be guilt-tripped into marriage, so the one who *is* in marriage love sincerely tries to wait indefinitely without pushing but the reward for their compassionate patience may well be seeing a wedding announcement in the paper with another's face in the photo where theirs should have been.

My best advice is to recognize when you are loved with the kind of love you seek and know how that love expresses itself in words and actions.

If you find yourself in a relationship where you feel it is time to marry and he does not want to, remember Michaela.

Michaela was a beautiful, brilliant college girl who was so popular the boys had to ask her out four months in advance to get a date. As she introduced the new members of her sorority to a nearby fraternity, a boy named Jim grinned and said, "But I want to meet *you!*" She smiled and gently guided him toward the reception line of new pledges, and he simply repeated, "But I want to talk to *you.*" She eventually agreed to a date. With patience and persistence, Jim won the heart of the famously sought-after Michaela. Then came graduation and the expected next step of marriage. She was career ready and so was he. Add one frugal apartment and you arrive at wedded bliss, walking the path of life together. Except Jim shocked Michaela, everyone else, and possibly himself by stopping dead when faced with matrimony.

You would have thought he was being asked to step off the edge of the Grand Canyon. Mules took notes on how to balk, watching Jim refuse to move into marriage. Perhaps the most important thing to notice is that *he never felt he was saying no to marriage.* He just wanted "more time." There was no definition of how much more time or why he wanted it, just pale panic at the thought of getting married.

He felt pushed. He felt compelled to bow the knee to societal expectations. He looked like a man who was moments from hearing the clang of closing prison doors. He looked ready to bolt. Eventually, he went along with the wedding plans but complained constantly. At engagement parties and meet-the-family events he said he felt as if he was being "paraded like a show horse." He didn't want to marry in a cathedral. Why couldn't their wedding be two witnesses and a licensed officiator? Engagement rings were rip-offs. Wedding gifts were unnecessary, absurd extravagances. The closer the wedding date loomed, the more agitated he became. Finally, after another desperate plea for more time, Michaela countered, "You mean you want to kiss it off!" For gentle Michaela, that was the equivalent of drunken-sailor cursing. For the life of him, Jim couldn't understand why she was so upset. She distanced herself from him, he missed her, they reconciled, and the date was set again. This time, he held on until the wedding was two weeks away before his panic became so intense that family members knew the bride would be at the altar alone unless the wedding was cancelled. Michaela called it off for the final time even though the wedding and bridesmaids' dresses were made and the invitations were sent. Jim continued to protest that all he wanted was more time and swore he loved Michaela. He actually felt hurt when she cut off communication with him for good and it was clear he thought she was the reason the relationship was over—not he. After all, he had only asked for more time.

About a year later, a friend of Jim's was dating a girl named Marnie. Jim was so smitten he asked his friend if he could ask Marnie out. His friend said yes. Four months later, Jim proposed and Marnie said yes. The wedding that promptly followed was a gargantuan event that packed out the biggest cathedral in Los Angeles. The bride's father was a wealthy medical doctor, and the wedding gifts purchased by his well-to-do friends and associates caused the housewares and gifts department of the biggest downtown department store to be back ordered. The gifts were heaped on long tables in Marnie's home, circling the living and dining rooms and stretching down the hallway, table after table laden with twelve-piece settings of pure silver and exquisite china, and other expensive tributes to their marriage. Jim happily attended engagement parties and accepted extended-family introductions, he and his twelve groomsmen rocked their tuxedos, the reception was massive, and the happy couple honeymooned in Hawaii.

Not one complaining peep out of Jim. Why? This time, he was in love.

Jim would happily have lived with Michaela for who knows how many years? Only when she began to edge toward marriage did he begin to edge away. It was a dance they could have done for decades. If marriage is what you want, remember Michaela and Marnie, and the man who was in love with both of them, but in *marriage love* with only one.

Beware: an awful, terrible, I'd-rather-not-tell-you-about-it truth is about to be revealed. Sometimes when a man buys an engagement ring, he is actually buying time. And silence. Women tend to invest an average of eighteen months in a relationship they want to end in marriage. A logic-brained man sees that an engagement ring will make her happy (translation: quiet) and extend their time together while pausing uncomfortable, confrontive "we need to talk" sessions about marriage. Some women settle for engagements that last for years without an actual date ever being set. Want to be one of them? Engagement marathons may end in a contentious separation followed by the man meeting a woman he falls in marriage love with and weds without hesitation. Think Bill and Kerry, Jack and Mandy!

Remember two things: marriage love is definitely a "thing," and your "good man" is not taken. He is out there, frustrating women by not being in love with them because he is going to fall in love with you—marriage love, I hope, if that's what you want. Mazel tov!

BE SELF-CENTERED

I spend a great deal of time in other people's business by mentally forming opinions about their life. I don't mean to, it just happens! During a short visit to the home of a friend I truly do love, I managed to think that his son's hair was too long and his lunch too sugary, their bathroom was a pit, and his video collection would reduce anyone to an idiot.

All this mental trespassing may seem harmless, but it becomes more serious when I am doing it in the life of someone for whom I consider myself responsible. Then it becomes a losing battle because the only life I can control is my own.

In raising my stepson, all my concern, my caring, the advice I gave, the boundaries I set, the chores I assigned, the homework I asked about, the rules I made—all were to help him get good grades, choose good friends, and prepare for educational and personal opportunities that would give him a good life. I simply could not have been better intentioned, and honestly no one could have been more diligent.

Then came the lesson. It was taught to me unsparingly by a young master of his own ship and captain of his own soul. I discovered I could make decrees, set limits, clarify expectations, inflict consequences, and you know what? He lived his own life. No one can control another person's life. If you want a crash course in both active and passive resistance, watch a child triumph over the combined efforts of parents, grandparents, the principal, the counselor, the coaches and yes, even their friends, to get them to graduate high school. I did. He was his own boy. Had he lived he would have been his own man. After he died at the age of 18 because he accepted a ride from a friend who was drunk, a friend I has warned him against, I suffered agonies of guilt thinking I had failed him. Then a wise counsellor uttered a sentence I needed to hear: "You tried to take responsibility for his life, and now you're trying to take responsibility for his death."

Sometimes the life of someone we care about is like a movie we can only watch as much as we would like to direct it.

In old-fashioned verbiage, we need to mind our own business. We need to be self-centered—in the sense of controlling our own life—and not other-centered. There is no more frustrating, doomed way to live than being other-centered. True, sometimes our business involves the lives of others. So be a wonderful parent but know their life is their own. Be a wonderful teacher but know the students are responsible for being wonderful learners. Lead the way but know you cannot make anyone follow. Jesus used to say simply, "Follow me." Then he kept on walking. Well, it would stand to reason that the author of free will would honor it.

BEAUTY VS LOVE

Beauty is over-rated, over-priced, and in time, over the hill. But the beauty industry has a vested interest in suggesting that beauty and love are linked, that beauty is the reason for attraction and therefore beauty is the foundation stone of love.

Accordingly, today's beauty industry has commercialized the face of love in my opinion.

Would it astound you to know that love has nothing to do with physical beauty? Thank God! We are not forever eighteen. My husband thinks I'm beautiful. He has thought so since he married me, and the sixty pounds menopause dropped with a thud on my body didn't change his opinion. Losing those pounds didn't change his opinion. He looks at me and sees beauty because the heart has eyes of its own.

But with cover girls smiling and movie stars glittering, we have an impression so deep it feels like truth that when a woman is beautiful, she will be loved. The weddings of beautiful actresses are gushed all over the magazines, complete with close-ups of their gigantic engagement rings. But look up People Magazine's "Most Beautiful" women and research their marriage history. Good heavens above, can it be that beauty has nothing to do with love or marital happiness? "But that's not possible," someone says. "*Everyone* knows the more beautiful you are, the happier and more loved you'll be!" If you happen to run into Everyone, tell them I said they are misinformed, which is a polite way to say they may take a seat among those convinced that the sun orbits the Earth, which is flat.

What we are talking about here is a belief that beauty is a necessary prelude to love, is a guarantee of love, or has anything to do with love. It may be a belief accepted by many, but it is still untrue.

Notice that love stories are not called "beauty" stories. And I'm so glad! Because I am about to share some love stories that are love stories indeed. Beauty is conspicuous only by its absence.

I was having breakfast with other singles at a seaside café when two people joined us. He was young and quite handsome. She was middle-aged, puffily overweight, her hair was brassy, and her roots were showing. She wore an Aunt Edna-knitted sweater either from or destined for the back rack in a used clothing store. The uncharitable thought occurred to me that if she ever wanted to marry, she would need to make some changes. Then I found out they were on their honeymoon. I learned the beauty/love lesson that day!

On a church worship team, the base player had the usual irresistible base player mystique. Young slender girls lingered at the music rehearsals to join the coffee shop gatherings that always followed. The worship team keyboard player was a middle-aged woman who weighed well over 200 pounds. One day, the base player proudly announced their engagement.

Sharon was a widow with six children. She worried about her age, her body, and her young family. "Who's going to want me?" was a question that haunted her. Well, I'll tell you who wanted her—a gorgeous Italian body builder ten years her junior, never married before, and so much in love with her he was honored to become not only her husband but a father to her children.

There was a young man in a certain church who looked remarkably like actor Tom Selleck. He was followed by adoring women not unlike a mamma duck leads a feathery stream of faithful followers. At the same church there was a girl who wore her hair in Pippi Longstocking-type braids and had a severely nasal voice with speech challenges. She was self-conscious and shy. Her friends were concerned about her ever finding a partner until Tom Selleck the Second proposed to her and she said yes.

Gwen was in a passionate relationship with her tall, handsome boyfriend. Then she was severely paralyzed in a car accident. Tom continued to visit Gwen in the hospital, "just affirming her as a person" as she recalls, but she couldn't understand why he would do that when the prognosis was a lifetime in a wheelchair with limited abilities. He refused to leave her. What he said is memorable. "You can date me, you can live with me, you can rent me, you can marry me. I'm yours." They married, and he has taken the most tender care of her ever since. He helps her dress and applies her make-up every morning. He loves her.

You don't need to be anyone other than you to be loved.

Besides, beauty is a slippery subject. It's a moving target through the generations. It's not only slightly subjective, it's entirely subjective! Just what IS beautiful? Are you beautiful? The "beautiful face" has measurable dimensions. If you would like to be informed and depressed at the same time, go to https://www.goldennumber.net/facial-beauty-new-golden-ratio and read about it. However, the definition of beauty alters with every generation and a little help from Hollywood.

The face of beauty is different with each movie goddess of the moment. The "perfect" mouth, eyebrows, lips, and body shape change constantly. In the early days of movies, actress Clara Bow had a tiny mouth with a sharply defined cupid's bow. Women drew that tiny mouth within the dimensions of their own and thought no one would notice. (Now, large lips are popular, and we draw bigger lips with lipliner and think no one will notice.) Then actress Joan Crawford rebelled and boldly applied lipstick to her entire mouth. She was brutally caricatured for it, but she set all women free, including the phenomenal, full-lipped Sophia Loren.

Pencil-thin eyebrows arched across the foreheads of Loretta Lynn, Bette Davis, and others until model Brooke Shields decided not to pluck hers. Recently, eyebrows morphed again, dominating foreheads in bold blocks.

The definitions of a beautiful body change, too. My mother had the slim-hipped, athletic body of model Cynthia Crawford, but she had it in the generation that gloried in the hourglass soft curves of Marilyn Monroe. Then she had a daughter (me), and I had Marilyn's curves in Cynthia's generation. God got a little mixed up, that's all. After all, He is very old. Then Jane Fonda introduced a home workout tape, and a nation of sweaty, smelly men's gyms resounding with the deafening clank of weights transformed into fitness centers where Lycra ruled and treadmills hummed and the feminine hardbody physique became a beauty goal.

Today, the demands of the beauty culture are intensified by our youth culture.

Every ad for a skin-enhancing product includes the verb "fight" as if a war against aging actually could be won. Evidently we believe it can because in 2020 we bought 49.5 billion dollars' worth of ammunition!* But believe me, youth can run away faster than moisturizer can chase it.

What is the root of all this aging angst? I believe it is the linking of beauty and youth with being loved. Why else would we go to such an effort to make forty the new thirty? Or fifty the new forty? I am positive there are bold women who don't allow anyone or any year to define them. The rest of us are all standing in line for the next complexion-transforming phenomenon because it hasn't occurred to us that we do not need to be transformed.

We juggle beauty routines to disguise whatever age we are, which is too old no matter what it is. I was in romantic Paris about to join some other young people for an evening out when one of the men took me aside, and with the concerned expression of a doctor imparting a sad diagnosis, informed me that a certain guy probably would not dance with me because he liked "younger women." I was twenty-four.

There is an attribute desired in actresses and models who become the face of a beauty brand. It means you think you can look like her if you use the cosmetic she represents. It is called "believable beauty."

My advice is to *believe in your own beauty*. Lady Clairol's tagline, "If I have only one life to live, let me live it as a blonde!" is the lottery-winning blend of envy (the grass is greener where the blondes graze) and insecurity (someone else is going to have all your fun) that makes us want someone else's beauty instead of our own. Millions of not-blondes raced to buy bottles that leached out their natural color. Thanks to roots, the repeat sales were guaranteed. It was a fantastic ad campaign. It's still working. Can you say "highlights"?

Believe in your beauty! Here is the intriguing part. You may never see it.

Your beauty may or may not be visible to you in a mirror because that is you *looking* at you. It is not you *being* you. You are so appealing, so attractive in person! You are life in action, all your joy and emotion and intelligence glowing out of you in beauty as you move through your life. You may never know how beautiful you are by being who you are. But everyone in your world will know. And they will think you're gorgeous.

So even when I can't see my beauty in a mirror, I know I have it. And I have proof. I have seen it in the eyes of those who love me. I am gorgeous!

[1] 'Revenue of the Cosmetic and Beauty Industry in the United States from 2002 to 2020', www.statista.com, 2019.

BULLYING

T hose who say that childhood is an idyllic time are air-brushing out the stuff that keeps counselors in business. I have one word for you: playground. It's an ironic word because playing is only one of the activities that goes on there. When the recess monitor is out of earshot, the horrific name-calling would astound many parents and send the "woke" population into seizures. On my son's grade school playground, I discovered that f**king f*gg*t was the epithet of choice. I was appalled.

Bullies aim for easy targets who have no allies. The shy ones, the sensitive ones, the socially awkward ones. Intimidation roars and stamps its feet, so you are afraid to fight it. But even if all you do is stand your ground, it may be enough. My mom proved that to me. Maybe she can prove it to you.

I thought her advice about a grade school bully was ridiculous when she first gave it to me. "Mom!" I protested. "I can't do that! She'd kill me! It would make it worse. Everyone would laugh at me." My persecutor was a girl who had discovered that I was easily flustered and didn't fight back. I know this because my mom actually asked her why she picked on me. "Because she gives such great reactions!" the girl grinned happily. Here is what my mother said to do and say.

"You just need to answer her back instead of getting mad. The next time Betty walks up to you and says something mean, look at her skirt in horror and say, 'What are those strings hanging down?' She'll look, and then you say, 'Oh, those are your legs!'" How can I ever articulate how much I would rather have died than risk my life uttering this lame joke that would plaster a bull's-eye on my back for the remainder of my school career? But I did it.

What happened? I said the words and stood there waiting for the social axe to behead me. Betty looked confused for a moment, then grinned and ran off. She never teased me again. My alternate nemesis was Sharon Striggs. Mom came up with another humiliating doozy. "Say, 'Let's all call her Scissors because she's such a snip!'" Oh, dear heaven. But I said it.

She stood there looking nonplussed, and then, as I live and breathe, one of the nicest girls in the school smiled and said to Sharon, "Hello, Scissors!" I was astonished! The Earth paused in its rotation. All the horses in the world raised their heads from grazing and looked toward our El Centro Elementary School playground. The sun blinked once. Sharon turned and ran.

Both of these girls became friendly toward me after our single confrontation.

I hear that some experts advise students to respond to bullies with gentle remonstrances such as, "Are you aware that you are hurting my feelings?" Since the answer is obviously "yes" because hurting your feelings is the bully's entire point, it seems counterproductive to point out that they are succeeding. For those who give the well-meaning advice, "Just ignore them," this implies that it is easy and will work. Actually, it's not easy and it doesn't work very well because bullies may be cruel but that does not mean they are stupid. In order to be untouched by bullying, you have to genuinely not care what anyone says to you or about you, and you must not show fear. Can a child do that?

This I know: most bullies aren't the invincible wall of confidence they seem to be. They attack safe targets. Don't be a safe target. Be someone a little unpredictable. Bullies don't want to risk embarrassment. Say something, say anything, and it may be enough.

The main point is to overcome the fear of saying anything at all.

I was so terrified of what a silly little schoolgirl would say, I cried at the end of every recess instead of answering her back. What in the world did I think she'd do? "She'd kill me" were the words I said to my mom. Our fear of a bully exaggerates them beyond all reason. After all, if they can stand there and be rude and the sky does not fall, certainly you can respond and the sky will remain in place.

What you say doesn't have to be brilliant. It just needs to be said. In fact, if you aim for a "devastating comeback," they will have to prove it didn't work by mercilessly mocking it and doubling down on their efforts to top it. Keep it simple.

"Seriously?"

"Aw, I'm gonna cry now …"

"You don't have to go away mad, just go away."

"Oh, ha ha."

"Good one. Not good enough, but …"

Anything will do.

If ignoring them works, great. But if it doesn't, don't keep your head down and hope they move on. If you keep your head down, they will be back. You were hurt, it was easy, and they didn't get any blowback. You're a source they will tap frequently.

Here are your choices—hurt them just a little or hurt yourself a lot. You are the one you are hurting when your silence agrees to be their victim. When you were born, the doctor didn't announce, "Congratulations! It's a doormat!" Say something.

Why am I talking about this in a book for adults? It's not only because some of you may be the parent of a bullied child. It's because just as little bullies may grow up to be big bullies, the downtrodden may stay in safe, passive ruts. Are you an avoider of confrontation? Do you call it "conflict" and avoid it at the cost of your personal dignity or professional respect? Then this chapter is for you as well. Life holds many "playgrounds" and there are bullies in every one of them.

Social media can become a voracious wolf pack, and kids can be overwhelmed and crushed by attacks from their peers. In our local high school, several students committed suicide after being subjected to relentless campaigns of ridicule, criticism, and condemnation. It was murder by mob, in my opinion. Then some incredible kids took action and started a counteractive movement to make every student feel welcome and important. That was their sane, merciful, and—it turned out—very effective response to the social media persecutors. These caring, brave students stood at the school doors every morning and greeted each person individually. They handed out affirming messages. It changed the social climate and mood of the student body. The suicides stopped. This embracing of the students was the "group hug" that made the difference between life and death for many of them, I have no doubt at all. Try it in your local school if social media poison is sickening the kids. When the acceptance and love come from the students who care, it means more somehow than having it come from the adults in charge. Our whole high school became a unified tribe, and the social media terrorists were shamed to silence.

You don't need to knock bullies out. You just need to knock them off balance. Self-respect is the beginning of others respecting you as well.

When I was ten years old, I kept my horse at a stable where it was all teenage girls. One sixteen-year-old called them together and for reasons I never knew, decided to make me their whipping girl. It lasted for months until she was kicked out of the stable, but it began with a remark I'll never forget. I arrived at the stable and saw the girls sitting in a circle where they had just decided to target me. I said, "Hi," and no one answered. I didn't know what was wrong, so I turned to Julie's old horse named Dusty and whistled lightly to him in greeting. "Don't whistle at him, he's not a dog!" she snapped, and the others laughed. I would give a great deal to be able to go back in time and reply, "Really? Could have fooled me!"

Better to respond than to surrender. Say something.

THE EXCEPTION There are schools so violent and vicious, lawless and dangerous that silence is the only thing that saves your life. If that is your situation, act accordingly.

CALLING ALL SEEKERS

"Gospel" means "good news." "Bible" means "book." Christianity has a simplicity to it. It is also a Grand Canyon-deep, galaxy-wide gathering of history, archeology, wisdom, prophecy, biography, genealogy, and a few other bookstore subject titles that would occupy you for decades. Or it can be as simple as "Jesus saves" graffitied under an overpass.

Some of the most ardent atheists who just couldn't stand the Bible and set out to debunk everything it said ended up writing literary defenses of it that are masterpieces of Christian "apologetics," which sounds like an apology but means an explanation. It is said that the Bible is an anvil that has worn out many hammers. The unbelieving best have led a charge against it in the battle of their spiritual lives, and in losing, gained the gift of eternal life.

Author and intellectual, C.S. Lewis (yes, he wrote the charming children's series about Narnia), loathed the sin-confessing Christians and ended up writing "Mere Christianity" which starts from the premise that there is no God at all so it's interesting to atheists and agnostics, and proceeds to logically deduce its way to the need for a Savior and offer a conclusion as to who that savior may be.

Josh MacDowell was furious and frustrated with everything pertaining to Christianity and the Bible, and he plunged into exhaustive research to prove the bunkhood of it all. His efforts morphed into the famous, "Evidence that Demands a Verdict" which presents the case FOR Christianity as it covers everything from the papyrus of the Bible pages to the complex prophecies Jesus fulfilled.

Here are more books that may interest the inquiring mind.

If science leads your quest and evolution is your question, John Wiester's "The Genesis Connection" may hold your attention. It compares the Biblical account of creation with the findings of scientific research on the origins of the universe and human life.

Just in case you can't tear yourself away from archeological digs, there is "Archeology and the Bible." There was an occasion where some people based their rejection of the entire Bible on a "mistake" they found in it: The Bible said there were camels at the time of Moses but according to archeology, there decidedly were not! Then a *new* archeological dig revealed there decidedly WERE camels at the time of Moses. They were in artistic representations of the time. Oh. Well, in that case … never mind!

It is interesting to note that the Bible cannot be updated, but science can. As new information changes what we know to be true about our world, science course-corrects itself. But the Bible does not have that option. More interestingly, it doesn't need that option. Before there were telescopes, the Bible said the Earth was a ball suspended in space (Job 26:7, Isaiah 40:22). Before there were microscopes, the Bible said to wash if you had touched a dead body (Numbers 19—ashes and fat are a primitive form of soap, by the way). Before "diabetes" was a diagnosis, the Bible said to avoid eating too much honey (sugar) or it would make you sick (Proverbs 25:16).

One time when I was considering other religions around the world, I went to the library and saw a whole shelf of books comprising the scripture of the Hindu religion. It surprised me that there were so many books! The Bible has sixty-six books, but they all fit in one book. So, I got the Jaws of Life and pried open my mind and said, "Open one of these books and read it a little." So, I did. I opened to this: "The earth is balanced on the back of an elephant in space." Well, that begs the question, what is the elephant standing on? Luckily, it gave the answer: four turtles. And THAT begs the question, what are the turtles standing on? Unfortunately, the answer to that was not given. (I just paused to confirm this memory by looking all this up and found that what I read was probably four elephants and one turtle ... it was many decades ago.) What does the Bible say about the Earth? It is a ball suspended in space. (Isaiah 40:22, Job 26:7) Science is betting on the suspended ball.

Buddhism has only about 1.2 practitioners in America, according to Wikipedia.org, but forty percent of them live in Southern California which brings a hint of fame to a religion that does not seek it. Perhaps that is why I know a little more about it than I know about Hinduism. The complexities of the Hindu deities are beyond me. I admit it. And while it is untrue that there are thirty-three million or three hundred million of them, they are numerically sufficient to leave me profoundly grateful for the simple trinity. Want to know more? Visit www.hindusinfo.com. I did.

At first glance, no two things could be farther apart than Buddhism and Christianity. Here is a second glance:

In Buddhism, "The process of rebirth (samsara) is driven by delusion and desire, with 'beings roaming and wandering on, hindered by ignorance and fettered by craving.'" (www.tricycle.org/magazine)

In the Bible, the Gospel of Luke 8:14 "The seed which fell among the thorns, these are the ones who have heard, but as they go on their way they are suffocated with the anxieties and riches and pleasures of this life, and they bring no fruit to maturity."

The Buddha (the universal being) could be said to have qualities similar to the omnipresence and ministry of God the Father, God the Son, and God the Holy Spirit. He is described as being able to manifest as everything from a chair to a mountain, and he helps seekers.

But those first-glance differences are acute. Buddhism advocates the relinquishment of all attachments and a "blowing out" of all desire, but from our mother's breast to our grandchildren on our knee, we are made for attachment. Life without desire is one definition of depression. Of course, if you are isolated and don't want anything you could be considered at peace, but it is also a rather excellent description of someone in their coffin.

Here is a puzzle for you: some find the Bible objectionably exclusive and Buddhism inclusive. But the Bible says that Jesus gives eternal life to anyone who believes in Him. Enlightenment, on the other hand, is so challenging, difficult, and elusive that humans must return and return and return in virtual perpetuity to try and get it right, and indeed, they may never succeed. That is not technically exclusionary, but if the qualifications are so nearly unattainable and the challenges so nearly insurmountable and you cannot achieve enlightenment until you succeed, it is about the same thing.

The absolutes of heaven and hell are offensive to some. Jesus referred to "the outer darkness" as the place where evil will be consigned. But Christ does not send people there. He said He is the light of the world and called out, "Come to me," in the marketplace and said, "Follow me," to potential disciples. Some did, some didn't. God is light. To choose to move away from Him is to consciously choose darkness. But it is our choice for ourselves, not His choice for us. Likewise, Buddhism does not force anyone to enlightenment, but without it, they suffer. The difference I see is that coming to enlightenment is something we do. It's an arduous process, and we may never achieve it. Coming to Christ is based on what HE has done.

It's a simple matter of believing Him. And ever since He said, "It is finished," our salvation and entrance to heaven have been achieved.

I see the Dalia Lama, his joy and peace, and think he is a lovely human being. But for seven years, Siddharth Gautama paved his path to enlightenment with horrific self-inflicted suffering and pain. It reminds me of priests who whipped themselves and wore hair shirts because the Apostle Paul wrote that he was "fulfilling in his body what was lacking in regard to Christ's afflictions for the sake of the church." (Galatians 1:24) These priests failed to notice that neither Jesus nor Paul afflicted themselves—they were beaten by opponents of the Gospel. Siddharth Gautama deliberately survived on one grain of rice a day, slept on nails, drank his own urine, and stood on one foot (which sounds easy but try it for five minutes—we don't make good flamingos). Then after seven years of this, he realized it was useless and stopped all the self-persecution. Those who were still into asceticism accused him of hedonism! Then after a night spent in meditation, he became the Awakened One—the Buddha. I hesitate to follow someone who took such an unnecessary detour for seven years! It just doesn't seem reasonable, wise, or useful to do what he did.

Buddhism is more a do-it-yourself program with occasional help from The Buddha and a more than fair chance that many revisits to this life are in store. Jesus offers to pay all debts for us, clothe us in His righteousness, come for us, and take us home. That is a huge and wonderful difference! The question is, do you believe Him?

It's not just believing IN Him, it is simply believing Him. I do.

Free will allows the mind to think, and allows us to decide. The first commandment literally commands us to think when it says to love the Lord your God with all your *mind*. Fortunately, we can love someone without understanding them completely—that is what all marriages are—so even though we cannot comprehend the greatness of God with our brains that will erase after ten minutes without oxygen and will return to dust after death, we can know Him and love Him. Jesus as God in human flesh (incarnate is the fancy word which is based on the word for "meat," hence "flesh") was an accessible man who lingered with the crowds and came to dinner in your home. He would heal anyone on any day of the week. He called His disciples friends.

So, it is about thinking. But most of all, it is about love. That is Gospel (good news) indeed.

1 John 4:10 "This is love: not that we loved God, but that he loved us and sent his Son as an atoning sacrifice for our sins."

2 John 1:6 "And this is love: that we walk in obedience to his commands. As you have heard from the beginning, his command is that you walk in love."

CALLING TO SAY WE'RE NOT
CALLING ANYMORE

I t's complicated. Love always is.

We've decided we are through. We've had it! We never want to speak to them again!

And we can't wait to call and tell them that.

No, we don't see the irony. It seems reasonable to call to say we have nothing to say. We might even call it "closure" because it seems official, but it's still contact. It seems legitimate but it is still wedging our foot against the closing door. We could let them know we have nothing more to say by not saying anything more, but we want to talk to them.

We don't see that we are manipulating ourselves into continuing the relationship by prolonging its demise. We make retrieving our toothbrush an urgent priority. We haughtily gather anything they left behind (old t-shirts, older CDs) and make a list of all the things we gave them or left at their place and arrange to exchange possessions. America separated from the Crown with fewer formalities.

We genuinely believe we are delivering a solid punch to their gut and striking a blow for our personal dignity by calling to tell them off. What we are really doing, of course, is clinging to the fraying emotional tie. "Goodbye" is the theme of a conversation we would not need if we had already left emotionally.

The problem is that no matter what we say, the message we communicate is that they still trigger our emotions. When we are genuinely through with someone, we are indifferent. We don't take little peeks at their Facebook page or other social media. We aren't thinking of where they might be at any given time of the day so that, funnily enough, we end up there, too.

Relationship books will tell you that if someone you are dating still has lots of arguments with their ex, it can be a sign that they are still emotionally involved with them. People you don't care about just don't trigger you very much. If they tell you that you're ugly and your mother dresses you funny, you reply, "So were you born with bad taste or is it a goal you've achieved?" You. Just. Don't. Care.

The emotion in a goodbye call reveals that it isn't goodbye at all. It's the outrage of being dumped, it's the frustration that your love isn't returned, it's a revelation of how much you are hurt. But most of all, it's grief.

The stages of grief are denial, anger, bargaining, depression, acceptance.

A phone call to tell them we won't talk to them anymore is a form of, "You can't fire me, I quit!" It's a denial of their dropping us. Anger? Of course, our phone call will be angry—how else can we tell them we never want to speak to them again? It's also a form of bargaining in that it opens the door to discussing all the issues of the breakup, even though we would swear it doesn't. It reveals how depressing our world is without them as they walk out of our life, and we follow them with our phone call.

Your call isn't anywhere near the last stage of grief—acceptance. You want to know what acceptance would be? Not calling them.

If you are going through this, what advice do I have as you seethe and want to dump their belongings on their front lawn after you key their car? Let me put it in a possibly appealing way. The best revenge, they say, is living well. So be a success at leaving this person behind. Keep your social media upbeat. If you happen to meet, say, "I hope you're doing okay." It will bother them more than anything else you could say because it infers they have struggled with losing you, and it also makes you sound caring yet indifferent. The exact balance you want.

When you love, the hardest thing to do is nothing, but it is the only thing that lets you heal. And as a nice side benefit, it is the only thing that makes a positive impression on your ex. It shows strength, a strong sense of self-esteem, and balanced independence. I promise you there will absolutely come a day when you don't remember where they probably are right now.

For "it" to be over, you must be over it. So, step over it and walk away.

And put down the damn phone.

CHILDREN ARE PEOPLE

"**W**ell, of course they are!"

I hear you, but that is not how we think of them sometimes. Some people think kids are human putty that we can shape—and, in fact, we'd better or we're bad parents!

True story: as the children were playing before tap dance class, one little girl cannon-balled through the chatting parents. Her mother made a desperate, failed effort to get her to behave, and then made a shame-faced confession to the other moms. "I used to think other people just didn't do a good job of disciplining their children. My son was so obedient and easy-going! I thought I was just a really good, effective mom! And then God sent me Bobbie!" Bobbie, of course, was the little hurricane who had just blown through the room.

It is so natural to claim good parenting skills when your child responds to them. It is so natural to feel a sense of inadequacy as a parent when your child fails to respond to them. I am suggesting that it isn't to your credit or your fault either way. You are a good parent doing your best. Your child is being who they are. Who else can they be?

Are bookworms made or born? Maybe a little of both. You can create a book nook, you can read to them and with them.

You can create the opportunity and live out the inspiration. They will love to read or they will not.

One of my friends promised her son that if he would keep at it, one day he would see the story happening in his mind's eye just as if he were watching a movie. He stuck with it, and one day burst into the room yelling, "Mom! I can see it! I can see it!" It was a wonderful moment in time. Another friend has one son who falls asleep when he tries to read, and a son who reads the Harry Potter books obsessively.

Are math wizards made or born? I understood arithmetic, then was forever lost in the maze that is algebra. I had to take it to go to college. I crawled through with a tutor and have no desire to confront a quadratic equation for the rest of my days. One of my step-grandsons does calculus problems to relax! It is not the fault of my parents that I am a writer and not a mathematician, and it is not to the credit of my step-grandson's parents that he is a numbers freak—I mean, someone who loves mathematics!

One mother remembered how her unborn son would move toward her hands if she put them on her stomach. He became a loving little kid who liked to snuggle. Her daughter, on the other hand, would literally move away in the womb if the mother touched her stomach. The girl grew up to guard her private space and didn't even like to be hugged.

Moms everywhere will tell you their children were born with distinct personalities fully formed.

Can you stop them from loving horses if their idea of heaven is a riding stable? (Me.) Can you coax them into a love of horses if they cry unconsolably when placed in a saddle on the pony ride at the fair? (My brother) My answer to both is no.

Can you make a kid eat something they hate? In grade school, I knew a kid who actually liked cooked carrots! When the cafeteria served them, we all lined up at his lunch table and gave him ours.

Kids are all so different! And yet as parents, we feel so responsible for their every action. It is impossible to mold human beings to our standards, preferences, expectations, societal dictates, or anything else. When it comes to raising your child, I'm afraid as a parent you're basically along for the ride.

I don't have to meet you to know that you will teach your child table manners and monitor their school progress. You will do hundreds and millions of things to raise them to be caring human beings who will be able to make a living, make a family, and make a success of their life. Of course, you will. However. People who are different in every way often grow up in the same home. The difference isn't in their parents. They have the same parents. The difference is in the people. And it was there even before they were born.

Choosing a Church

A church is not a building. Church (from the Greek word ekklesia) means an assembly of people. So, when you choose a church, you are really choosing the people. And I'm including the church leader(s) among those people.

To say "churches are different" is the understatement of the ages. Even among Bible-based churches, there are differences. Rather than define them all, let's leave a few trees standing and say that "worshipping God in spirit and in truth" (Jesus' words) can be done in different ways.

You are looking for a place where you can ask, seek, knock, grow in understanding scripture, gain spiritual strength, and share your journey with others making the same journey. One of the original names for Christianity was The Way. You're looking for a place to lead you along The Way and love you always—when you are true, open, closed, willing, stubborn, and basically, a human being learning to walk with God. In Eden, God walked with Adam in the cool of the evening. Jesus walked with His disciples.

Don't miss the fact that you are also called to extend compassion, mercy, and patience to others, so it's important that you like these people! I mean it! If they don't open their hearts and their homes, think twice.

Church is not a building you sit in for one hour a week. Seeking God and seeking relationship with his other children is the most natural thing in the world. And you will need friendships—not just a pastor whose sermons/talks you enjoy. Staying the same is so nice, especially when you are comfortable. Growing can be a bit more arduous. Growing in Christ sounds gauzily spiritual but it can mean being fertilized, pruned back, and watching some well-loved weeds pulled up. You will need the fellowship of your church.

You're looking for a compassionate, wise leadership who doesn't covet power and protect it by forming an iron wall of elders flanking one nearly-worshipped pastor. There should be spiritual growth all around you, with people discovering spiritual gifts and callings, and given opportunities to minister and serve and put them into practice. It is called "growing in Christ."

The worship should touch your heart and stir your spirit, which doesn't mean it's perfect musicianship—it means the Spirit of God ministers through it. You will know the difference. It's not about professional CD perfection, and it's definitely not about just listening to the terrific worship team with your hands in your pockets. It's about you worshipping God through music, just as you worship Him through prayer, through reading the Bible, and through serving others. Worship is life.

I grew up as a Catholic until I was eight years old because my grandmother was Catholic so Mom accommodated her. Then my spiritual future became unmoored until I turned sixteen and it was decided that I should be something definable. So my Dad said, "We'll enroll you in an Episcopalian confirmation class because they let you believe anything you want." (My apologies to the Episcopalian church!)

In these two noble denominations I learned to love Jesus and think organ music was the only acceptable kind because guitars and drums in worship were abominations unto God. Well, almost. Today I'm sure most of their congregations are strumming away lightning-bolt free, but this was a long time ago. (It is a testimony to God's sense of humor that I ended up playing the guitar on the worship team of non-denominational churches.)

As for their use of hymnals, my experience was that the choir knew the songs, but the congregation did not. We rarely sang the same hymn twice. We all dutifully held the hymnals, but since ordinary folk can't read sheet music, we had the words but not the melody. We meandered along behind the choir and tried not to sing too loudly because we had no idea what the tune was. The songs were written for the soprano (high) range. Altos and second sopranos (me) did our squeaky best to hit those high notes which seemed to be in every hymn. Over the years I frequently wondered why the church powers-that-be didn't notice their congregation struggling to figure out the melody and hit the high notes. On occasions like Easter and Christmas when familiar songs were sung, the whole congregation bellowed happily and praised God indeed, but the next Sunday we would again be fumbling through an unknown hymn.

As for following the service, for me it was a frantic shuffling back and forth of pages in The Book of Common Prayer. It was a beautiful, wonderful book! But the service was dotted with things like Collects. A collect is a special prayer written about a specific subject. Collects are available for each Sunday in traditional form on pages 159 to 185 and in contemporary form on pages 211-236. By the time I made it to Page 181, everyone had said "Amen" and moved on.

I finally gave up trying to flip back and forth and settled for listening attentively.

In my church, a simple thing like raising your hands to heaven in worship was first frowned at, then grudgingly allowed, then furtively tried, then finally accepted as a sort of "red-headed stepchild" in worship.

Let me say loudly (I'm typing really hard) and clearly that the above was my personal experience and opinion only. I respected and revered the high church denominations but somehow felt like a spiritual misfit.

Then a gentleman introduced me to a "spirit-filled" church. Everyone knew the songs and sang them with joyful love for God. They lifted their hands and when I hesitantly tried this, it felt like a child lifting up its hands to a parent to be held. I loved it. Sometimes I felt tremendously prompted to share a thought from God and discovered I functioned in the kind of prophecy that gives encouraging messages to the church. I discovered that putting your hands gently on someone's shoulder and praying for healing was a "thing." I had a cyst on my hand that disappeared in about sixty seconds. I loved it.

However! I visited another "spirit-filled" church and was shocked at what I perceived as silliness. One of the Scriptures says to be drunk with the spirit, not alcohol. This was interpreted by one man as staggering and weaving down the center aisle, only to snap out of it immediately if someone needed to walk past him. Another man unaccountably took off running at full speed and rocketed all around the inner perimeter of the church. Someone explained to me it was because the prophet Elijah once took off running to beat a storm and ran ahead of a chariot and horses, and this was a manifestation of that spirit. The pastor preached into a microphone attached to towering speakers. His voice blasted out and it hurt my ears! Then one of the faithful explained that the Bible says to praise God in a loud voice. But they didn't have microphones and monstrous speakers back then. They were referring to a natural voice. Then came the moment that I raised my hands in praise and the whole congregation saw my nail polish. Suddenly I felt soft hands on my back and opened my eyes to see four sweet women around me quietly praying for my salvation because of that nail polish. Actually, I had been previously warned they thought make-up and jewelry wrong, so I had minimalized my make-up that day out of respect, but I simply forgot about the nail polish! Oh dear. Hell, here I come.

I had to conclude that not all churches which acknowledged and functioned in the gifts of the Spirit (hence the adjective "spirit-filled" church) felt right to me. But my own church was right where I needed to be to grow.

My advice on choosing a church is this:

Choose a church according to their doctrine. Usually they have written material on it.

Choose where you are spiritually comfortable. Perhaps a quiet church where you can be anonymous in the back row and observe, taking it all in, is just where you need to be now.

Perhaps you want a large, active, growing congregation with classes and groups for all ages and stages of life.

Perhaps you will be drawn to a very small church where the teaching hits home and the people are nice, and you are known and loved.

Perhaps you are like I was, a dolphin looking for a sea to joyfully splash around in, and you'll flourish in a church that lets you grow in the gifts and go deep into fellowship.

Jesus made it so simple. He said, "Follow me." In following Him, we trust that He is leading. He said to ask, seek, and knock and we would receive, find, and the door would be opened. If you are asking Him for a church, let Him lead you to one.

And remember. The church means the people. The building can be a small apartment where a Bible study is held. Someone invites you to it when your life is at a lonely place and you are seeking without even knowing. You lose the apartment number but follow the sound of singing.

You find a small bit of heaven on Earth. Someone there invites you to his church and it becomes the church you love. That is how it happened with me.

May it be so with you.

CLEARING OUT THE ATTIC

There you are standing in the middle of a room packed and stacked with boxes of memorabilia, looking around vaguely and feeling as if you don't know what to do. You feel that way because it's true—you don't know what to do! After all, you are not only faced with deciding what *you* want to keep, you must decide on behalf of *others* what you think *they* will want to keep.

Standing in my own storage room, I was knee-deep in everything my parents valued enough to save. I was supposed to decide if their great-grandson, now five years old, would want to have it. I was supposed to sift through the last earthly presence of these two people I loved. How could I discard any of it without feeling as if I were erasing them?

I thought it simplified things that I have only one niece who has only one son until my brother said his grandson wouldn't be very interested in his great-grandparents because he never met them. Does my brother have a point? To me, my grandnephew's great-grandparents are "mom and dad." But too my grandnephew, they are ancient history. It doesn't take long for a person's life to drift out of emotional reach.

What can you tell me about your great-great-great grandparents? Oh. How about your great-great grandparents? Me neither. What about your great-grandparents? My mom shared a few stories her mother told her about *her* mother and there are a few photos, but that's it. I have no emotional connection to my great-grandparents. Maybe my grandnephew won't either.

No matter how you choose to decide, every single thing you pick up still requires a decision. It's emotionally and mentally exhausting! I went through storage containers crammed with a vast assortment of things. Zillions of photos. So many letters! So many cards! An ancient projector and a box of home movies in silver containers. Scrapbooks, baby books, photo albums, journals, jewelry, christening clothing, a Daughters of the American Revolution silver spoon from my maternal grandmother (no, I didn't join). Massive scrapbooks of my mother's glamourous life, as she and her sisters toured the world in an adagio dance team before she became a Rockette. Diplomas from my father's professorial career, the original manuscripts of his books typed on a manual typewriter by my mother with complex, endless footnotes (if that's not love, what is?), on and on and on. Is your head spinning? Mine was.

My dad kept a pair of baby sandals they bought me in Mexico. I picked them up, holding a memory of myself, but it wasn't my memory. It was his. It was a mind-bending moment. What should I do with them? (My baby shoes only mattered to my dad. My niece might have treasured her dad's baby shoes, but mine? I let them go.)

The bottom line is this. If every generation in your family passes on everything saved by the previous generation, imagine the storage units your great-great-great grandchild is going to have to rent. Someone has to let things go sometime. And apparently that someone is you.

Here is what I discovered. Before it's about deciding what to keep or pass on to others, this is about *you*. This is your time. So, take your time. Take it all in. Read everything. Handle everything. Allow it to be a slow, savored experience. You are browsing through, paging through, and revisiting your life.

Be prepared for your emotions to regress as the edges of time soften and your heart and mind go back. I looked up from reading letters hardly able to believe I couldn't just pick up the phone and call the person. You will feel happiness, sadness, longing, and even old anger may raise its head. The past is not Pandora's box but it may not be a Tiffany box either.

As I did this, I easily threw away a great many things that were nice to see again but I could tell once was enough. It was easy to put all photographs into one box. I could also make obvious decisions like putting my brother's baby book into the box destined for my niece. I ended up with several trash bags of things I discarded and a few boxes of things to pass on, and it felt great!

Then I went through it all again. Yes, again. My mind was clearer the second time. I was able to throw away even more for one very good reason. As I went through my personal memorabilia the first time, I reviewed it carefully because I hadn't seen it for decades. The second review revealed whether it held my interest still. If I found myself buzzing through something impatiently, that was obviously something I was already done with!

It took as long as I thought it would take (a few weeks) but it was so good to stack just a few plastic containers in a discreet corner. I have no doubt that when I go through it all again, I will throw away more. But the urgency to get rid of things will be gone because a few containers never hurt anybody. Someday when my time comes, the contents of my plastic storage containers can simply be transferred to trash bags. Done! My lifelong correspondence received from close friends is separated out to mail to them so they can leave it to their children. Their letters tell their life stories.

Your memorabilia is your journey. Keep what you enjoy reliving.

COLLEGE AND CONTENDING FOR THE FAITH

I didn't lose my faith in college but I was lousy at defending it. After all, if you're raised in a home where a vague idea of God and church is shared by one and all, who is going to challenge your faith?

It's all so simple and so clear until someone challenges you. One day they ask, "Did you know that the Ten Commandments were just copied from the Code of Hammurabi?" Well, no you didn't know that. Is it true? No one ever said that to you before!

Then someone smugly remarks, "Did you know that Jesus never said, 'I am God'?" What?! Now that just *can't* be true! Replying, "He did too!" sounds like a preschooler who needs a nap but it's all you've got. So, you call your pastor and ask them. They sound patient and understanding, but sometimes they don't exactly know either! They may say Jesus expressed it in ways that the people of the time understood. Great, but you need to find a place where He expressed it so you can tell it to the atheist in your science lab. The Pharisees were trying to kill Jesus because He made Himself one with God but where did He say it?

Want to know? Here it is: "Before Abraham was, I AM."

John 8:56-59 *(Jesus says to the Pharisees) "Your father Abraham rejoiced at the thought of seeing my day; he saw it and was glad."*

"You are not yet fifty years old," they said to Him, "and you have seen Abraham!"

"Very truly I tell you," Jesus answered, *"before Abraham was born, I am."* [59]At this, they picked up stones to stone him, but Jesus hid Himself, slipping away from the temple grounds.

The reason the Pharisees promptly picked up stones to kill Him was because they understood what He had just said. *He had said He was God.* Only God can say I AM. God told Moses that "I AM" was His name for all generations. It means you are outside of time, always in the present with no beginning and no end, from everlasting to everlasting. You and I cannot say I AM because we have a birth date and will have a death date. As a man, Jesus was temporarily within time. As God, He is eternal.

Now if someone says to you that Jesus never said He was God, you have an answer! But sadly, I must tell you that once I found this answer, I shared this clash and confrontation of Jesus and the Pharisees with an atheist I knew. I read it out loud with the expectation that he would at the very least find it meaningful. He listened. He shrugged his shoulders and said, "It's just a difference of opinion. You find it in all literature." If all he heard was a difference of opinion, he couldn't hear it at all. Jesus called certain people spiritually deaf and blind because they were.

It might be important to note that I never sought confrontations. I didn't wear a cross or carry a Bible around with me or have a Christian bumper sticker. I never brought up the subject! But I was a magnet for hardcore unbelievers. One gentleman from my church who brought many seekers to the services couldn't understand why I never brought anyone. "Did you tell them about the blood of Jesus?" he inquired, incredulous.

How could I tell this dear, simple man that the kind of people I met on campus didn't care a fig leaf for the blood of Jesus?

I heard it all. Jesus was just "one of many ascended lights." Lots of people were named Jesus—his name wasn't special. The Bible was filled with false books because the Council of Nicea had removed all the true books and put in false ones. Jesus got all his knowledge from a secret trip to the Middle East. The Bible had thousands of errors. I didn't know how to answer these people! The ones who were angry or dismissive were bad, but the amused condescending ones were the worst. With a knowing twinkle in their eyes, they would practically pat me on the head when they said, "Christianity is a good baby step."

One professor listened to a discussion of Jesus and gave a long, slow nod of his head. "Jesus was a good man," he said. And then he changed the subject. When I shared my embarrassment and frustration with a youth pastor, he listened. Then he said gently, "Keep contending for the faith. That's how you learn." But he didn't sit me down and give me the answers. Why not? He must have known what I know now—I had to do it myself. It means more when you come across the answers yourself. The answers you find are more than answers for others; they build you up in your faith. I thought contending for the faith was fighting those who came against it. Now I see contending for the faith as contending for MY faith. Those who confronted me in my college years weren't really asking questions about my faith. They were informing me it was misplaced. The Commandments, the Bible, Jesus—they thought I was wrong about all of them. In reading the Bible through the years, I learned my faith was placed in the right Person so I can say what Paul said in 2 Timothy 1:12 "I know whom I have believed, and am convinced that He is able to guard what I have entrusted to Him (my soul) until that day."

My advice?

You can't fence with someone else's sword. You need your own. And you need it to be sharp. Go to any bookstore and line up their Bible versions on a table, all open to the same Scripture in the New Testament. Read that Scripture in every version. Buy the Bible that makes the most sense to you. That's your sword.

Keep it sharp.

CRAZY LITTLE THING CALLED LOVE

I was in a book club once where I discovered that the men were often married to women who didn't really understand what they wrote. Their wives weren't enthusiastic readers and not particularly deep thinkers, whereas their husbands were intellectual wordsmiths. I mentioned this to a friend who asked, "What about you? Your husband doesn't read much, and he doesn't know anything about your field of corporate copywriting!" I hadn't even thought of that. Our roundtable of authors married people who thought the library is where you go for peace and quiet to look at the pictures in your magazine.

Why is this? It may be about balance. Two fun-loving people who avoid responsibility may co-create a future that is a lot less fun. Two nose-to-the-grindstone people may miss a lot of joy. Two spontaneous spenders may end up with too much month left over at the end of the money. Two penny-pinchers may live on lukewarm gruel by candlelight to create wealth but never be comfortable enjoying it.

We need balance for financial, mental, emotional, and even physical health. I'm lucky if I can operate an egg timer. I got a camera and couldn't open it to reload the film.

I hung a Roman numeral clock upside down and wondered what was wrong with the numbers. I am ridiculously incompetent. On the other hand, I'm a great magazine writer! My husband is a fix-it guy who can build a backyard deck and assemble furniture. He can barely write a grocery list. Am I married to the perfect guy or what? He never worries, so I worry less. He is never afraid, so he makes me brave.

Let's applaud marrying your opposite! It works well. Together, you create one balanced life. And that isn't crazy at all.

DON'T TRY TOO HARD

There are about a ka-jillion advertisements out there (or maybe it's fantastic-a-tillion, I don't recall the exact figure) selling you things to make your weight lower, your lips fuller, your stomach flatter, your complexion smoother, or make your hair either more of what it is (fuller, thicker, shinier) or into what it isn't (blonde if your hair is dark, straight if it's curly, and curly if it's straight).

One implication of all these appearance-enhancing product ads is that your appearance needs enhancing. Their combined effect on self-image can be intense. One young man married a beautiful young woman who didn't want him to see her without make-up. "I'm so ugly!" she exclaimed. He was astonished into silence for a moment, then gently said, "You're beautiful!" He was up against years of influence that had convinced her she wasn't. He did his best to persuade her she looked so gorgeous without make-up that he actually preferred her that way. Do you think he succeeded?

Ads are in the business of selling, not communicating deep truths about love. The truth is you are beautiful and lovable just the way you are! (You don't believe me, do you? Keep reading.)

I know a woman who owned a beautiful wine bar. She was successful, smart, and funny. She looked her age. When she was widowed, she made a bold decision to move to a new area. A gentleman who lived down the street looked at her and saw her intelligence, sense of fun, and energy, and fell in love. Her eyes had lines but he thought they were mesmerizing anyway. He did not marry someone twenty years younger. He married her. Last seen, they were grinning like teenagers as they vroomed off on his motorcycle into marital bliss. Perfect beauty had nothing to do with either one falling in love with the other, and I can testify that their eyes practically crossed in romantic delight when they looked at each other.

Beauty is not what we see, it's how we see it. We don't think someone is beautiful because they are beautiful, but because we see their beauty. Love sees beauty in the beloved.

In my life, there have been many men who did not know I existed, and that was quite an accomplishment considering how hard I tried to prove to them that I did. And there have been men who were smitten, captivated, and in love with me, yet I was the same person!

They say finding the right person is a case of being the right person, and I would add that being the right person means being yourself. Everything you are will seem beautiful to someone who loves you. And that matters because much of what you are physically will change. Good health is not guaranteed, and age *is* guaranteed. Someday your skin will lose collagen, and your breasts will give in to gravity. But when someone loves you, they love you. They love you well, they love you sick. They love you young, they love you old.

We live life in person. We cannot be an air-brushed version of ourselves. Be your beautiful self and marry a man who sees the sunrise in your eyes whether you are wearing mascara or not.

"DON'T YOU THINK ..."

A dvice that begins with the words, "Don't you think ..." actually means, "*I think* ..."

"Don't you think *you* should... a) go to bed earlier, b) ask for a raise, c) get a haircut, d) eat more vegetables, e) drink less coffee, f) declutter your closets," all mean *they* think you should. It just sounds more persuasive to gently coo, "Don't you think you should ..." rather than bray in your face, "I think you should!"

It can feel surprisingly uncomfortable to respond, "No, actually I don't think that." It feels confrontational. It instantly erases all the camaraderie of "Don't you think ...?" which assumes you two are thinking alike in cozy agreement. Your honest response can feel as if you just built a fence between the two of you and you're both locking and loading conversational weapons on your respective sides. It feels that way because that's what often happens!

Try saying, "No I don't think that," and you may hear, "I'm just trying to help!" (a statement so devious it earned its own chapter) or "Fine!" Which means it isn't.

If you have a friend or family member who prefaces their thoughts with "I think," treasure them! They make it an even playing field. They have a brain, you have a brain, and you're both verbalizing your thoughts.

"If I were you …" is also a bit of a nudge because it implies very delicately that what *they would* do is what *you should* do.

There is an underworld of possible implications beneath those simple words, "If I were you …" Most of them would put a hatchet-chop end to a friendship if spoken out loud. Here are a few unspoken things revealed:

"If I were you, I'd pack up his stuff and leave it on the front lawn … [but you'll probably go all mushy and cave in and not only NOT pack up his stuff but wash and iron it to prove that you really do luuuurrrrvvvvvve him, you co-dependent doormat!]"

"If I were you, I'd pack up his stuff and leave it on the front lawn … [that is, if I actually had someone, which I don't, and possibly my tendency to leave relationships on the lawn is the reason I don't have someone, but I'm damned if I'll admit that because it's more fun to make you feel as bad for having a relationship as I do for not having one.]"

"If I were you, I would tell him to … [Of course I'd never have that much nerve, but you'll never know that because I like people to think I'm a lion when I'm actually a ferret.]"

"If I were you …" really means, "If I were in that situation …" and is meaningless because you are two entirely different people. The implication is that they would make a better "you" than you do, which is irrelevant even if they're right. An honest statement would be, "I actually don't know what I would do in your situation, much less know what you should do in it." But that feels so unhelpful, doesn't it?

Perhaps we should all just listen and let people talk their way to their own solutions. That is what counselors do, and they get paid lots of lovely money for it! But since you are talking with a friend, you're happy to do it for free. Unless you make them pay for your coffee and croissant.

EVERYBODY'S A CRITIC

If you've ever floated a creative concept in a marketing meeting, you know how it feels to watch it sink. Even if it manages to bob up again by the meeting's end, it gets a good dunking first. Why is that?

Everyone in a meeting is there to contribute. That is the value they bring to the conference table. If an idea is suggested and all they say is, "Great!" then all they have contributed is approval. It is viewed as more intelligent and more powerful to critique an idea than to praise it, so their contribution in the meeting becomes finding a fault, a flaw, a reason why it won't work. If they can't come up with a great idea, they share the credit for someone else's idea by adding a course correction to it.

Here is a real-life example of this odd dynamic. An airplane company wanted music for their ad campaign. This was in the pre-digital days when many people were involved in the recording process. A studio of live musicians was expensive. When the new theme music was presented to a conference table of executives who knew nothing about music, silence reigned as they listened.

One of the attendees spoke up hesitantly, "What was that jingly thing?" A tambourine, he was informed. "Oh. I didn't like that."

The musicians were summoned back to the studio to record it again. At the next presentation, another random comment was made, and it was back to the studio yet again. By the time all the executives had spoken, there were nine recordings of the theme and the man in charge of the process had had it. He came to the next meeting, played all nine versions, and asked them to make a decision. Guess which one they chose? Yes. The original version. He didn't tell them they had done this because it would have restarted the whole process, but he did communicate the final results to the company's CEO who swore him to secrecy about the ridiculous financial debacle. He didn't share the story until half a century later when the company no longer existed—possibly because none of its customers liked "the jingly thing."

If they can't find an objection to correct, it's very effective to infer that just one customer could even remotely take offense to your idea. This is viewed as saving the brand from losing customers. If you squint, you can see this written on every rung of the corporate ladder: "If you can't come up with a great idea, get credit for shooting one down for a great reason."

What if the original idea was better in its original form? We will never know how many astonishingly excellent campaigns were presented and rejected or modified beyond recognition.

What is my advice? Many creatives deliberately put something objectionable in their creation so reviewers can reject it and feel competent and important while keeping their grubby paws off the rest of it. Other than that, you can try letting the critical comments run their course. Here is how that works:

You present your project and sit back. As it goes around the table, dutifully stabbed by every Brutus seated there, you will want to defend it. Don't. You will want to save it. Don't do that either. Allow it to be soundly refuted, found wanting, judged objectionable. Let their satisfied silence linger. Do not be the one to break it! Soon someone will speak up in slight, ever so slight, favor of your project by objecting to one of the objections! They will do it gently. "Actually, I don't think our customers would leave in thundering herds because we said, 'Think healthy!' I know, George, you thought it insulted them by implying they're junk food junkies, but health is kind of a thing now, you know. And we do, you know, kind of sell health products."

This statement, believe it or not, will put spurs to everyone else in the room to object to the other objections and brilliantly prove why they don't apply! It often happens that by the end of the meeting, everyone has decided to give your idea a try. The difference in their minds is it is now *their* idea to champion your creation, rather than being "yes men" to your championship of it.

If you are a person with genuinely creative ideas and products, you might consider avoiding the corporate structure entirely and going into business on your own. But that takes the courage of a visionary. If you have it, go for it.

Walt Disney was firmly informed by some potential project investors that adults don't want to go to a playground for grown-ups. What an absurd idea! An absurd idea that became Disneyland because Walt Disney knew about the ageless child in all of us. He was also firmly informed that cartoons were for children so no adult would want to watch a feature-length animated film. Another absurd idea! When "Snow White," was presented at the Radio City Music Hall in New York City in 1937, it was held over for so long—packing the 6,015-seat theater at every showing—that the other theaters waiting for it complained. Radio City had to release it even though they were still selling out.

Everyone's a critic. Be like Walt. Be your own cheerleader.

FINDING YOUR PURPOSE

Sometimes finding your purpose seems a slightly vague pursuit and sounds like something that requires sitting in cross-legged isolation on mountaintops for an eon or two. The good news is it may be going on in your life right now and you just haven't noticed.

Your purpose is what you find yourself drawn to and engaging in even though you might not literally say it's your "purpose" or your "passion" to anyone who asked you about it. Here is how it might look:

You may notice that instead of avoiding hospitals and sickrooms you gravitate to them and want to give the sufferers a hug and a smile and tell them they will get better soon. You cry for them when they don't. You have natural empathy and infinite patience for the healing process, and it gives you joy. That's your purpose. You may work in Hospice. You volunteer everywhere there is human suffering. You are an ambassador for God and don't even know it. Mother Teresa said her mission was to go out and "find Christ in all his distressing disguises." So is yours. You may choose a health-related career as a result.

But it might not be that way. Your purpose and your career may not be linked. This might be your story:

When the dangers increased in your town, it broke your heart to watch the news and see kids so wild and lost and angry. Instead of using your savings to relocate to a safer place, your reaction was to hit the streets armed with a basketball. You've always relaxed by shooting a few hoops, and you relate well to teenagers (a unique characteristic in and of itself since so many adults are absolutely flummoxed by teenagers) so you put together your relaxation pastime and your affinity with teens, and there you are creating peace in your community by organizing basketball games after school in troubled neighborhoods. Your day job is just a job. Your purpose is to befriend the isolated, unmoored ones drifting the wrong way. Looking back, you can see it. Scouts. Little League. Big Brothers Big Sisters of America. It's always been all about kids! You've just never thought about your concern and love for them as your purpose. But it is.

On the other hand, just because you're good at something doesn't necessarily mean it is your purpose. A person may be good at many things they have no particular interest in. One father whose daughter was astonishingly gifted at tennis put her on that career path and found that she didn't have enough interest in it to pursue it! He was first astonished and then disappointed, but he was powerless to make her care. She was magic and magnificence on the court and could have played her way straight to the top. But she didn't want to.

One way to discern the difference between an ability and a purpose is to be aware of the effect the activity has on you. Do you lose your awareness of time? Do you notice you aren't looking at the clock? Do you forget to eat because you don't get hungry, as opposed to making snack runs every thirty minutes because you're restless and bored? When I was writing this book, every day I woke up to a hint of Christmas morning in the air. I was excited to fix coffee and resume writing. As I wrote, I would unintentionally tune out the world around me and lose track of time. Living your purpose immerses you in the experience. It is quite different than putting in a dutiful eight-hour day.

Your purpose may make itself known in your teens or your eighties. You may have many purposes over the span of your life. Life is long, and we change along the way. You mav have one purpose that you fulfill in different ways over time. At the age of ninety-nine, evangelist Billy Graham no longer travelled around the world but continued his ministry through prayer at his North Carolina home.

I was a writer from the time I could pick up a pencil. I wrote poems on cards to my mom and dad. My school compositions were always marked with an "A" and a teacher's note: "Very good—if you wrote it yourself." It was a compliment and a slight at the same time. Teachers doubted that I could write as well as I did without parental input. But I could.

The day I knew I would write for a living was in seventh grade. We were assigned a book report. In class one morning the teacher asked us to turn them in, which was the moment I realized I had forgotten to write mine! I grabbed a piece of paper and a pen, and as the teacher collected everyone else's, I madly scribbled mine. The next day when I came to class, there was writing all over the blackboard. It looked oddly familiar. It was my book report! I was equally thrilled and horrified as she stood there and read it out loud, no less, and said it was an example of how a book report should be written! It was a book about a wild horse, and all I can remember was my flamboyant closing line: "He went on to live in untarnished glory among his own kind." How horses go about tarnishing their glory, I was fortunate in that no one asked me. I kept that book report in a scrapbook, but many years later it embarrassed me to read my seventh-grade writing so I threw it away. I wish I hadn't.

One of the smartest people I know had a different experience. She was a steady student but had no preference for any one subject. Her room was always impeccably neat, and more than that, it was very organized. Who would think an organized room was a clue to a great career? But it was! She became the top administrator in a major west coast law firm and made it look easy to keep a large staff consistently efficient. She found great fulfillment in working with Hospice. She discovered that the practice of yoga resonated deeply with her spirit, and she became a teacher. Her well-organized (of course!) Gentle Yoga classes are actually quite complex but are experienced as seamlessly simple. She plans them with aging bodies in mind. Her sessions are so crowded there is barely room for participants to lay down their mat. Her Zoom class has thirty to forty people in attendance!

There is a golden thread of purpose shining in her life. It is comprised of compassion, spirituality, and organization. There is "going with the flow" and "going with the grow," and she is an example of both. Look for the common denominator of activities in your life and you may find you are right on track with your purpose.

In case you're interested, biblically speaking, our human purpose is basic and very do-able. Micah 6:8: "He has shown you what is good and what is required of you. To do justly and to love mercy and to walk humbly with your God." In the Book of Ecclesiastes, the writer was an incredibly rich, wise man who had stood atop many of life's achievement mountains where we climbers think we will find happiness and fulfillment. He reported the view like this in chapter 3 verse 12: "I know that there is nothing better for people than to be happy and to do good while they live. That each of them may eat and drink and find satisfaction in all their toil—this is the gift of God."

Some people—the lucky ones, some say—know their purpose early on. They also know what career they would like to develop. For the rest of us, my advice is to be an observer of your life and take your soul seriously when it communicates either its happiness or unhappiness. Don't settle for distractions, time wasters, or sedation as ways to handle a sense of misdirection or unfulfillment. You are truly the best guide for your journey! Follow your talents and your passions, and you will end up living out your purpose.

And if your purpose in life is only one key occasion where you light a candle in the darkness because you are the only one who has a match, well done! Everything that leads up to having that match is part of your purpose.

I have mentioned author Gwen Cooper elsewhere in this book, and her experience applies here too. She was a published author. She loved cats. These clicked into sync when she took home a blind kitten whose story became her book *Homer's Odyssey* which went on to be an international bestseller and not only change the lives of cats around the world and help animal shelters in wonderful ways, but inspire the wounded and the challenged to boldly live joyful lives. Homer had a purpose too, and it was linked to Gwen's purpose—to change the world for the better. If a cat can do it, we can too.

FOR THE LOVE OF A CAT

If you love cats, you may be called a "crazy cat lady." It's supposed to be a joke but it's also a judgment. You have to resort to cat company? You're sublimating your love into cats? You're crazy. There are men who love cats, but for some reason only ladies who love cats are called crazy.

I think it disparages a person to say that they "sublimate" their love when they give it to a pet. It is fair and right to love animals. After all, Adam had his first relational experience with God and his second one with animals. According to the Bible, up until the time the Earth was flooded and all vegetation was ruined and the animals were given to us as food, we were vegetarian and the animals were not afraid of us. You could pet a deer, hug a lion, and all was well. I wish we still could.

In fact, I think the "sublimate" label also disparages the pet! Animals receive love and give love no matter how many scientists mock what they call anthropomorphism—attributing human emotions to animals.

Magazine articles and books are written on how to comfort people through suffering. Cats can't read. These books are for us. We need them to know what to say and very often what NOT to say. "Don't tell them your comparative experience. Don't give advice. Never say, 'Well at least …' and fill in the blank with a situation that would be worse." Lots of people say their cat "helped them through many tough times." Their presence is the loving one we need to comfort us without words getting in the way.

Our kitties stay by us when we are sick. They don't even turn on the TV or read. Love is what they are doing. One cat lay next to his ailing human and kept his paw on her shoulder. One woman wrote that her migraines kept her in bed or on the couch, and her cat didn't simply stay with her, he would gently give her kisses on her forehead. He would lie on the back of the couch behind her head and gently touch just the tips of her hair. She said, "It was as if he knew my head hurt." I think he did.

During difficult times, our beloved little friends let us talk. They let us hold them and cry into their fur. When the world is lonely, they are glad to see us come home every day. We wake up to their friendly, furry face. It is their quiet presence, their faithfulness, their devotion during the ordinary days, the best of times, and the worst of times that makes our hearts so empty and yet so heavy when they must leave us.

I once wrote a poetic tribute to dogs. It says that when we get married, we promise to be loving no matter what, but we often struggle with keeping that promise. The last line is, "The ones that succeed have four paws and a tail." It goes for cats too.

My advice? Don't let anyone pet shame you. Ever. To love and be loved is an honor and a joy and a privilege. Always. We are called "crazy" for loving our cats? We would be crazy if we didn't.

Four Paws and a Tail

Amazing how something with paws and fur,

Sometimes a lovable tail-wagging cur,

Sometimes a pure-bred worth every penny

Can love more than most, loving us more than any

Amazing, such love! Who could resist?

Who else would we let lick our faces like this?

Who else would we let interrupt when we eat

To 'share' so often we have to reheat?

Does anyone covet our company so?

Is any so glad to see us come home?

Do any just listen without their advice?

Who quickly forgives when we aren't so nice?

Love such as this, we promise to people

With preacher intoning beneath a church steeple.

But keep such a promise? We try and we fail.

The ones who succeed have four paws and a tail.

GET "OUT THERE!"

You'll never find love unless you get off the couch and get out there! This advice sounds logical, but is it true?

First of all, notice that you DO get out there even if you couch-binge when you're at home. You go to work, and if you work with the public, technically you're "out there" all day meeting people. Do you stop by your local coffee haven each morning and shop for groceries every week? That counts! So, when people push you to get out of the house, they are really seeking to drop-kick you into the world on your precious days off! Oh, the unkindness of it. Not only do you have to put in a forty-hour work week earning your daily bread, you have to leave the comforts of home on weekends to wander the world in search of attraction and connection, neither of which you have any control over at all.

It's true that being alone does effectively preclude being with others, and commuting between the couch and the kitchen all weekend will not place you in the path of someone new. But going out is no guarantee of meeting someone either! However, the reasoning of the couch-ousters is, "You never know, so get up and go!" and they have a point. After all, although it is technically conceivable that your refrigerator will die and the person who comes to repair it will be the actual heir to the family appliance empire and the two of you will fall in love and get married and move to Monte Carlo, I doubt it—don't you?

My approach is to modify their advice a bit.

Consider the timing factor.

I met my husband when he left the state he lived in and moved to mine. Then one day he walked into my church. The sound of my jaw hitting the floor is still reverberating in the choir loft. He was a tall, handsome Italian with a smile to melt all morals (Not that he melted mine, but you get the idea.). Before he relocated near me, I could have attended every dance within a thousand-mile radius every weekend and never met him. So don't run yourself ragged going out all the time. Of course, one could always say the ONE time you stay home is the ONE time your beloved will show up so you MUST go out EVERY time, but that "must" will wear you out. It's a scenario usually brought up by those who were very tempted to stay home one evening, didn't, and met someone wonderful. Generally speaking, if you live a balanced life of activities you love combined with well-earned rest, you will meet someone else doing the same. I did.

Don't smoosh your jigsaw-piece self into a space that won't fit.

In your efforts to "get out there" don't do social contortions that distort who you really are. If your idea of perilous heights is adding the star to the top of your Christmas tree, then don't force yourself to enroll in a wall-climbing class where you meet a diehard hiker who dreams of Everest, and the two of you end up taking separate vacations the rest of your lives. It will upset the family dog.

Don't try too hard.

Men say they know who they want to approach within seconds after walking into a room. I think women do too. A person's essence attracts you before they say or do anything! Don't mess with your essence! You can skew your first impression by doing an impression of someone you think will make a good impression.

Don't put yourself through your version of hell in your efforts to "get out there." I advise that you increase your chances of meeting someone compatible by enjoying this world in the ways you would like to enjoy it. If you are practically a still-life portrait of someone reading, just think of all the kick-boxing classes you can avoid and still meet the love of your life! Conversely, if a sweat-gushing workout and a sports challenge that dislocates important things that probably shouldn't be dislocated are your idea of euphoria, just think of all the head-bangingly dull books you can avoid reading! If you're talking to the right person—which is someone like you, who will like you—an opening line of "So what's your resting pulse?" is just as good as, "Dostoyevsky's psychological themes just slay me!"

Investing hours, days, and months into activities that bore you stupid or put your body through athletic indignities you loathe will leave you resentful and frustrated with the process and vowing, "I will" to someone you actually will be saying, "I won't" to for the rest of your life after you forsake all faked-enthusiasm activities and become the true you. But if you're doing things you love, the time is well spent even if it doesn't end in love. Let joy be your reason for "getting out there." Go give the world your beautiful self. Being surprised by love is more fun than besieging it like a closed-drawbridge castle. Be you and go have fun.

A Note on Dances (and Museums)

On every bright-idea list of where to meet people, I find dances and museums. Now I am positive that many eyes have locked across dance floors through time. However. A friend of mine wrote these words on her ticket to the ninth-grade dance: "How to be a wall weed without really trying." For me, dances were opportunities to watch the boys dance with shorter girls. If you are going to sulk in the restroom or lurk behind the drapes glaring hostilely at the punch bowl until it's 10:30 pm and you feel you have served enough time to be paroled and go home, don't go to dances. Go do something you enjoy!

As for museums, there are many frequented by crowds of knowledgeable, well-educated people. I also know of many where visiting them will only disturb the spiders. But I have yet to hear gales of laughter or ripples of flirtatious conversation drifting from *any* museum doors. Usually, a hushed silence reigns and everyone is nose-deep in a brochure or focusing on the artifacts. But for the sake of the exception, I will suppose that there could be a magical museum moment when a handsome archeologist will brush the dust of the tombs from his hat as he takes it off and introduces himself to a woman who has pried herself off her couch and is dutifully "out there" pretending to be enthralled with an Egyptian mummy. So if you want to museum-hop, go for it! Handy hint: in the famous Louvre museum of Paris, the Mona Lisa pick-up line is, "She looks smaller than you expected, doesn't she?"

P.S. At one dance, a good-looking young man noticed a woman standing beside the punch bowl looking around the room and seeming happy to be there. She stood with a crutch because she was one-legged. He thought, *What an amazing woman!* and he walked up to her and introduced himself. He was awestruck. Now he's married to her. This postscript is not about challenges or prosthetic devices. It is an observation that being yourself is the right person to be in order to attract the person who will love who you are. Life says, "Come as you are!" So does love.

GRIEVING

There's always hope. Except when there is death. That is the pain of it. That is the frustration and anger of it. That is the infuriating helplessness of it. You can do nothing. They are gone. You are still here.

I have learned that grief is not the same in every loss. I've experienced the death of my first husband, my parents, and a stepson. In losing my husband, I learned some things that might help you if you must go through the loss of a spouse.

Before my husband died, if you had asked me to describe stages of pain from the most minor to the excruciating, it would have been something like this: discomfort, pain, agony. After my husband died, I discovered that "agony," a perfectly adequate word before, didn't even touch—let alone describe—the pain I felt. I couldn't stand it. I couldn't bear it. The only reason I did was because I kept breathing. I wasn't suicidal, but I wanted to die and be with him again.

Ultimately, I came into an understanding of why it hurt so badly. When we marry, we become one. Our bodies join together in physical intimacy from time to time. Our spirits are somehow joined all the time. When one of us dies, there is a moment of soul surgery. There is an incision made from the collar bone to the pubic bone, and its depth goes through to the spine. They are separated from you. It is stitched up, and oil is poured on it. And the first words you hear are, "Get up and walk."

A friend told me that the morning after his abdominal surgery, the nurse asked him to stand up and walk a few steps. He thought she was kidding. She wasn't. Evidently, the faster you are up and moving, the better for the healing process, physically speaking. Spiritually speaking, it is the same. However, that doesn't mean you immediately force yourself to live as if you were not in deep grief. It just means to recognize that a journey through the valley of the shadow of death has begun. Keep walking, and you will leave the valley someday.

You don't move on. You are moved on.

It is like this:

You are at the beach and decide to play in the waves. You look back at the shore to note where your beach towel is. After standing in the cool water for a while, rising and falling with the incoming waves, you glance back at the beach, and someone has stolen your beach towel! Then you look back down the beach and there it is! But how could that be? You haven't moved. You've been standing right there all the time! But you did move. The currents of the sea gently moved you along and you weren't even aware of it. Time does that. It gently moves you along and you find yourself in a different place emotionally and mentally.

And it is also like this:

You are standing on the beach. You look up and see a tidal wave looming over you. There is nothing you can do, and you just stand there and let it break over you. Time passes. You look up and see that the waters have subsided a little and are just over your head. Time passes, and you look and see the water is at your neck. Time passes and you see it is at your waist.

Time passes and it is at your knees. Time passes and it is at your ankles. You walk away.

I knew I was beginning to recover when I thought of my husband one day. When I thought of him, I realized that in order to think of him I had to have *stopped* thinking of him for a moment. You see, my husband was constantly on my mind no matter what I was doing. I didn't know how to feel in that telling moment that meant I was beginning to heal. I wanted to stand forever at his grave, yet I wanted to love again. I wanted to remain his widow yet I missed the joy of marriage. Who was I becoming?

Letting go.

You don't let go of things. They let go of you.

Here is how it happens:

My husband's bathrobe smelled like him. I treasured it. Every once in a while, I would hug it and breathe him in. Two years later, I realized it did not have his scent anymore. It just smelled like a bathrobe that needed to be washed. So I did.

At first, you save everything they ever touched. Don't pack away, give away, or throw away things because you think you should. I took down all our photographs two weeks after the funeral because a friend told me I should. I took off my wedding ring because I thought I should. There is no "should."

The thing I saved the longest was his favorite t-shirt. Then there came a day when his favorite t-shirt became just a t-shirt. That is the day I let it go.

Time, time, time.

It takes more time than you want it to.

Think of it as you would a physical injury, and it may be easier to understand. Let's say you break a leg while skiing. Yes, the doctors set it in a cast, but the doctors don't heal your leg. You don't heal your leg. Your leg heals.

The spirit is like that. It heals. There is no particular activity that speeds up the healing process.

It takes time to phoenix up out of the ashes into a new person. The eventual becoming of your new self is the end of your grief.

You walk through the valley of the shadow of death (Psalm 23). You don't stay there.

There will come a time when you heal. Healing is not forgetting. It is living your life as it is now.

Let's revisit the ski slope. Your leg has healed, and you're ready to ski! Would you go immediately back to the most difficult run? Probably not. Be patient with yourself regarding relationships and new life challenges.

When is the time right?

You can't run away from grief, but once grief begins to fade, you can't stay with it either. Changes and new things will happen and will feel right. Trust yourself, and make decisions just as you did before.

My Parents

I mentioned the deaths of my parents. I missed them both in different ways and it surprised me. But wouldn't you miss different people in different ways? The part of losing them that was difficult was deciding what to do with everything in their life that they left behind.

If I considered throwing something away (the last handkerchief my mom ironed for my dad) it felt like I was throwing my parents away. You may feel like that too.

My advice? Give. I gave to the grandchildren what I thought would have meaning or usefulness to them. I gave to Goodwill things that would benefit others. I encouraged myself to let things go by realizing that everything I kept would have to be thrown away by someone else after I go! It is not erasing them to bestow or let go of their belongings. It's honoring them. The fact that it is difficult honors them as well.

My Son

I saved everything. I admit that getting rid of it will have to be done by someone else. I packaged it all neatly so it won't be difficult for them.

The Bible says that grief lasts for a night but joy comes in the morning. The night is a long night, but our world turns, so be sure that the sun will rise upon you. Because it will.

HE'S JUST USING YOU

If you want her to break up with someone who is using her, do not ever say these words to her: "He's just using you."

There are ways to help someone who is indeed "just being used," but telling them they are being used will backfire and blow up in your face. When you advise her to leave him because "he's just using you," she will respond by increasing her efforts to be loveable in order to prove that you are wrong and she is loved. Her need to be loved is what got her into a one-sided relationship in the first place.

Because she passionately wants to prove she is lovable, she gravitates toward a "user" who gives her endless opportunities to prove it. All her efforts are doomed to failure because her partner chose her specifically because of her need to please. He needs to keep her trying to please but falling short of it so she'll continue to try. She can never do enough to prove she loves him because the game is to keep her trying to earn his love.

Her need to be loved will keep her struggling to make the relationship work. If she admits she is a convenience or a bank account or a verbal punching bag, her dream of love dies and she suffers the perceived shame of being unworthy and unwanted. She doesn't want to admit that his love is a lie because she thinks that proves her unlovable.

Worse, if she takes your advice and refuses to be used, she will be dumped. And that will prove to her that she is unlovable, and possibly goad her into blaming you that it's over.

If you want to save your friend, help her realize how wonderful she is instead of trying to prove how unloved she is in her current relationship.

She could give some thought as to why she believes she has to work to be loved. You might also explore the psychological dynamics of user personalities so she can recognize them and perhaps become aware of what she likes about them—what attracts her to them.

Users choose their partners with merciless accuracy. They are sharks who can smell blood in the water. They can hear a wounded fish thrashing in the water from miles away. In human terms, con artists can spot an easy mark.

An abusive man goes for a vulnerable, co-dependent, people-pleasing woman. An abuser calls a woman a "bitch" not because she is one, but because she isn't. An actual bitch would never allow herself to be called one. He knows perfectly well his humbly compliant partner doesn't deserve the epithet, but he also knows she will double down on her efforts to prove she isn't a bitch, thus providing much entertainment in his definition of that word. She will do anything for him and take anything off him in the quest to prove she truly loves him. She may even allow him to kill her. It's a terrible thing.

Sometimes your friend isn't in a relationship with a dangerous man, just a selfish man who is content to use her as long as she allows it. He gives booty calls, not flowers. She is a last-minute option in his life, and one that can be cancelled at the last minute as well. She is a default, not a first choice. Still, telling her she is just being used can bring out all of the behaviors noted above. It is still more effective to talk to her about *her* than about *him.* She is wonderful, worthy of respect and devotion. Self-respect inspires respect from others. Keep it positive!

If your friend is locked into one of these relationship dances of death, the key to her freedom is within herself. After all, "self" esteem cannot, by definition, be how someone else esteems you. It is all about how you esteem yourself. Your friend needs help, serious help, and this chapter can't contain all she needs. But now you know what not to say, and sometimes that is the first victory in a long battle.

Never say, "He's just using you."

How to Invite Single People
if You're Married

Invite singles the same way you invite your married friends. Why do I give this apparently obvious advice? Let me take you back in time to my single days at church.

Mark was one of the kindest, nicest guys ever. He was an elder in our church, and he often gave the announcements between worship and the sermon. He stood at the podium and said, "As you know, this Thursday is Thanksgiving. So, if you have no family and no friends, no plans, nothing to do and nowhere to go, the Smiths are opening their home and you can go there."

I am not exaggerating. I wish I were. He smiled and sat down comfortably in the front row as an embarrassed silence descended upon the congregation. Mark was happily clueless.

Paraphrasing him in a later phone call to my brother, I declaimed, "Hail, ye great unwashed and unwanted! If you have no family, if you have no friends, and you are all alone, the Smiths have, in their infinite pity, decided to make the ultimate sacrifice and leave their front door open so you will have somewhere to hide your uninvitedness."

On another Thanksgiving, I was thrilled when the Vanderlynns invited me to dinner! I liked them, and I was both honored and pleased that they would ask me. I brought flowers and a dessert box of chocolates. As we were chatting in the kitchen, I thanked the wife for inviting me. She said, "My husband and I asked God who we should invite for Thanksgiving and He said we should ask you and our neighbor." Until that moment, I thought they had invited me because they liked me and wanted me to join them for Thanksgiving. It turned out I was a name on God's charity list.

Because I had accepted the Vanderlynn's invitation, I had to turn down a few others (from caring people who had volunteered to hang the single social albatrosses around their necks) and I solemnly swear they all said the same thing in the same words. One patted me on the arm and looked woeful as she said what they all said, "We just wanted to make sure you had someplace to go." Somehow, I don't think that is what they said to the actual friends they had invited for Thanksgiving.

Without meaning to, married people treat single people as the "other." The inviter and their friends are the "us" and the single is the "other" invited to join them. They sometimes say they have friends coming over (the "us") and if you have nothing to do, you can join them. This implies that they issued a social invitation to friends, and you (the "other") can join the "us" if you have no other alternatives. Gee, thanks. They use words like "include." "We'd like to include you" means they and their friends are the group, and the single is the "other"—an outsider.

This tendency to tag on the words, "… if you have nothing else to do …" is done with the best of intentions. What they mean to imply is that the single is socially happy and busy, not staring at four walls and worrying that God has chosen them for a life of celibacy. Unfortunately, the words carry a hint of, "If you do have something else to do, by all means do it."

My question is, how do they invite their friends? "We'd love for you to come over for dinner Saturday. Are you free?"

Now you know how to invite a single person!

HOW TREES GROW

One day, as I drove through a high pass where pine trees blanketed the mountains, I noticed something.

Trees normally grow straight up from flat ground. But the mountain slopes were very steep. The pines did not grow straight out from the slanted mountainsides. Instead, they sharply angled and grew UPWARD toward the sun.

I'm sure there are botanical reasons for this. A flower seems to "follow the sun" as a result of the lengthening of certain cells in the stem throughout the day. But there is a lesson as well.

No matter what you grow in or where you grow from, aim for the sky. Respond to the sun. Grow upward. Pay attention to heaven in plotting the course of your life. Look up to the light.

If you're born in a situation that won't respond to normal actions, do the extraordinary. The mountainside trees weren't born on nice, flat ground. They were born on an impossible slant. They did an extraordinary twist toward the sun and grew anyway. You do the same. Then someone like me will notice, and they will do it too. And someday a mountain range of sun-facing trees will be your legacy. And that is your destiny.

IGNORE THE ODDS

Most of my success was achieved by being ignorant of the odds against it. In fact, all of my success was achieved that way. When you have a contribution to make to the world that only you can give, the odds don't count.

Let's say you want to write a book. You can feel the writing energy building. That book is *in there*! You can't forget about it. Disappointing others is bad, but disappointing yourself is worse—a snub to your own soul. Sometimes you don't even know what a book is about until you start writing. Creativity is a wild child. You can't parent it. You can only give it birth.

If you're curious about the odds against a book being published, I'll tell you what they are. Huge! Happy? How are you going to use that information? It's only good for discouragement, which means a removal of courage just when you need it! Even if the odds are in your favor, it will make no difference because giving your gift and fulfilling your creative destiny are imperatives, not sensible choices.

But there are better reasons for ignoring the odds. Who makes the odds, anyway? They are gleaned from statistics, such as, this is how many authors seek publication and this is how many authors achieve publication, therefore here are the odds against your book being published. Odds do not factor in genius or a writer's voice that captivates readers. Your book may be the cream that is going to rise to the top, but statistics are not able to prophesy, only to guesstimate.

And speaking of odds, who makes the judgments on what to publish? Have you ever looked up the discouraging rejection letters sent to eventual best-selling authors? It's quite cheering!

Author Gwen Cooper wrote a book called "Homer's Odyssey" about her extraordinary, courageous, inspiring, blind black cat named—yes—Homer! The publishing industry rejected it at first with the supposition, "No one reads books about cats," without first publishing any books about cats because no one would read them. Circular reasoning at its worst! Thank heaven Gwen kept writing. Would you like to read her book? It's a worldwide bestseller in twenty-two languages. Homer has encouraged wounded veterans in their recovery, emboldened physically challenged people all over the world, inspired millions of readers to lead a brave life, and endeared himself to a readership who loves him to this day. His brave little life is still changing lives. This effect could have stopped with Gwen herself, but she ignored the odds and kept writing and gave the world her Homer. Be like Gwen.

Even if your odds-ignoring bravery doesn't result in worldwide acclaim, it's a rush when your creative expression sees the light of day! When I walked into the MCA recording studio and heard my simple guitar vocal tape of my first published song transformed into an orchestrated recording, soaring on violin wings as gorgeous harmonies poured out of gigantic speakers—wow! Here's how it came about. My brother knew a fair amount about the music industry. I only knew I liked the music of singer/actor Dean Martin (Who? Look him up.) and wanted to write a song for him. My brother's mind boggled at my confidence born of ignorance and he tried to save me from my absurd ambition. I'd never get a song to Dean

Martin! In fact, getting a song out at all was a near impossibility. Disc jockeys at top radio stations, he warned, kept a large cardboard box nearby to toss in an average of five hundred unsolicited CDs sent by singer/songwriter hopefuls every week. I listened very nicely, then turned over a Dean Martin album where I noted that his producer was Jimmy Bowen at MCA music, and I called him.

Three weeks later, I had an appointment with the under producer Duane Eddy (the 50s Twangin' Eddy legend) who screened unknown talent, and three months later, several of my songs were published and one even got an advance! My brother didn't know whether to be happy for me or drive off an overpass in frustration that my ignorance had resulted in bliss. No, Dean Martin didn't record my song, but I was a published MCA songwriter just the same. And my professionally produced song (four of them, actually) was a thrill!

On the other hand, my brother's daughter wanted to be an actress. He stood protectively between her and a future doomed to fail. Did she know, he implored, that Los Angeles was wall-to-wall with young restaurant servers with similar ambitions? They worked and worked out, thronged to cattle-call auditions and ultimately aged out of most roles, hemorrhaging hormones as they disappeared into their unfilmable fifties with no money in the bank. She decided against hitchhiking to Hollywood, not because of his dire pronouncements but because she ultimately didn't want to. She's happy. That's not selling out or giving up. She is being true to herself. Be true to you.

So, what do the odds mean to you? Nothing. They can't stop you. Only you can stop you. Only you have your gift to give to the world. If you don't give it, no one else will. No one else can. They are not you. Statistics are useful in measurable, pragmatic matters, but creativity refuses to fit on spreadsheets or kneel to formulas. In any creative endeavor, ignore the odds. They do not apply. They can't.

What if you don't make it to the top?

What is "the top" for authors? The Pulitzer? The best-seller list? There are many best-seller lists. Is it being on a list or at the top of the lists? Staying on them for a certain period of time?

Don't let comparison be the measurement of your success or you guarantee your own unhappiness. So how do you measure success? I'll answer that with a better question. How do you celebrate it? Celebrate your success as it arrives in whatever form it comes, and you will enjoy it. Compare it, and you will tarnish it. Put a shade over its light. Diminish it. But most of all, you will dishonor it.

What if you DO make it to the top?

Actors who receive the Oscar say the "high" lasts a few weeks only to be replaced by pressure to repeat the success the next year. The excitement of goal-attainment passes like a Christmas morning once all the presents are opened. Yes, there is that moment at the pinnacle with horizons expanding in all directions, and there is applause, praise, and sometimes money. Then our nature as future-oriented beings sets our feet on the next journey. It's true that the joy is in the journey. Don't rob yourself of your joy. Enjoy your journey.

Give it wings!

By all means, do all you can to share your gift with the world. Just never look at the odds while you're doing it. There are many ways to publish and promote creations, and they feel like work because they are. But every parent joins the PTA, so bake the cookies and show up. When you hold your gift high and feel it lift and leave you, you will experience the humble ecstasy of the creator. You'll watch as it rises into the sky and becomes a speck melting into the blue, bound for glories beyond the horizon of you. It will have a life of its own. And the odds can go home and have a consoling cup of hot cocoa.

I'm Only Trying to Help

This phrase—this washing of the hands in innocence—might have been the first thing the devil said when God caught him messing with creation.

Let's say your spouse observes you folding towels and corrects the way you are doing it. You continue to fold towels the way you've always folded towels, and they snap, "I'm only trying to help!" But saying you need help can only imply you are not doing very well at whatever you are doing, so you are offended and they are huffy.

They feel that their "help" is being rejected, repudiated, repulsed, and refused, and their little feelers are tweaked.

You, however, feel disrespected, belittled, condescended to, corrected, and judged.

Most of the wars in history were fought for fewer reasons.

"I'm only trying to help" puts you in the impossible position of having to change how you do something or risk offending the suggester who will then imply that in addition to being incompetent, you are a stubborn, over-sensitive towel wrecker! After all, they were ONLY trying to HELP.

You were innocently folding laundry. How did you end up in divorce court? Because it isn't about the towels.

My first husband observed me preparing stew for dinner and said to dice the vegetables in bigger chunks because it kept the flavor in. I dodged a bullet by simply doing as he suggested. Years later, after he went to heaven where he is undoubtedly telling the angels how to cook the Marriage Supper of the Lamb, my second husband observed me dicing vegetables for stew and said to make smaller chunks because they were easier to eat. I'm an easy-going person and didn't really care one way or another so I complied. HOWEVER, if a delivery from your local pizza place follows a domestic disagreement wherein the allegedly over or under-diced stew ends up in the dog's dish because you're too mad to serve it, you are not alone. And it's because you heard the subtext so clearly: "You obviously are earning a 'D' in Stew-Prep 101. You need help." Stew becomes more than a dinner. It is now the tip of the iceberg to the Titanic of your marriage.

Why, exactly, is "I'm only trying to help" such a crazy-making statement? Because it makes them look good and you look bad. It makes them look innocent and you look guilty. It makes them look kind and you look mean. It makes them look generous and you look unappreciative.

If they are helpful, and you won't accept it, what does that make you? Confident? No, it makes you someone who overreacts and makes a big deal out of nothing; someone egotistical and headstrong. Look at how many labels are slapped across your forehead! Resist the labels and they multiply! You are rude. You are hurtful. You are unreasonable.

"I'm only trying to help" is an accusation that makes you defend yourself, and then they label your defense as an attack.

There are three manipulations lurking in "I'm only trying to help." They are "only," "trying to," and "help."

"Only" implies they "only" did a tiny thing, a good thing! You, however, insulted the universe by rejecting the help it sent to save your sorry self.

"Trying to" subtly suggests there is good to be done and they are "only" doing their best to do it. Resisting someone trying to do good is bad, right? "Trying to" also implies that it is a necessary thing for them to do and they are making a noble effort, whereas you are being unaccountably uncooperative.

"Help" is a word of many wonders. It's a selfless, generous, positive, good-Samaritan word. How could "help" be wrong? Well, it could be wrong if it wasn't requested or is unnecessary. And it could be wrong if the "help" is the result of one person overvaluing their opinion and undervaluing the opinion of someone else. And it could be control in disguise.

Rephrased, "I'm only trying to help" becomes "I'm telling you what to do." It's a wolf in sheep's clothing. There are sharp teeth involved. You can tell by how hard they bite when the "help" is refused. So, is it an order or a suggestion? Do you have permission to refuse it? By bleating, "I'm only trying to help," they position you to apologize and comply. If you refuse, it defaults to a fight.

Admittedly, I'm a pretty easy-going person. But once in a while, the "helpful" people are pitted against each other rather than against someone obliging like me, and the result is quite entertaining!

One of our friends was as bossy as my first husband was. While I was preparing the burger patties for a barbecue, my husband noticed the size of the patties and "helpfully" said to make them larger. I up-sized all the patties. Then our bossy friend came in, surveyed the patties and "helpfully" said to make them smaller. So, I downsized all the patties. My husband came in while I was doing this and protested.

Utterly delighted, I summoned our controlling friend and said to the two of them, "You want the burgers smaller, and you want the burgers larger. I will make them any size you two decide they should be." With a flourish, I folded my arms and stepped back. Both began with smiles and patient explanations as to why their way was better. When both rejected each other's advice, they quickly tensed into tight smiles and sharper phrasing, and the discussion blew up into an earth-tremor argument with each accusing the other of the same character flaws. The entire gathering ended up in the kitchen to watch the show. Each combatant consigned the other to a life of unreasonable stiff-neckedness and went to different rooms in the house to sulk, and I don't remember how the burgers ended up. But I had a great time!

If you want to decline suggestions, you have to develop the hide of a Texas armadillo to the responses you'll hear. "Why are you taking that attitude?" is their most common reaction to your unfathomable disinterest in their superior knowledge. Oh, how I wish there were words to convince a "helper" that they have an attitude of their own, but no words will do that. "Okay fine! Do it YOUR way!" is an exit line with ominous "to be continued" overtones as your bull-headedness is sarcastically commented on in perpetuity.

If you are married to a diehard control freak—oh pardon me, I mean "helper"—it's honestly easier to follow their suggestions if you don't care either way. If the "helper" is your mother-in-law, going along with her directions during her visits will keep your husband from having to referee between the woman who endured the agony of giving him birth and the woman who endured the agony of giving his children birth.

But there are things you can try.

Give them a reason that is not reasonable but is based on emotion or loyalty. You'll be surprised how that helps by making them feel less challenged by you. You can say to them, "That sounds right, but this is how my mom taught me to [cook stew, change toilet paper, fold towels, mop floors, handle temper tantrums, etc.] and I just feel so disloyal to her when I try to change it. I'm sorry! I hope you don't mind too much."

That last sentence tends to effectively close the subject because it implies so many things and positions your "helper" where you want them to be—out of your way. It implies that you're going to do it your way even if they do mind, but they are so important to you that you hope they don't mind "too much." It positions them to take the high road of not minding "too much" since no one wants to *admit* to minding "too much." It also allows them to be technically right, as you imply that the reason they will mind you continuing to do it your way is because their advice is so excellent. It also implies you are suitably sorry and regret their discomfiture and appreciate their understanding. They get to feel superior, patient, kind, forgiving, and noble, and you get to blow off their suggestion. It's a win-win.

You can be vague. "You're right (in a wryly humorous tone) but you know me!" You can take a chance on follow-up questions. Sometimes they work! "Will it make you mad if I don't?" followed by a neutral shrug. "It's just my way of doing it. I hope you don't mind too much."

You can be elusive. When they say, "I'm only trying to help," you can smile and coo fondly, "I know you are!" and keep doing what you're doing.

No matter what happens, you can at least know you are not crazy to react to "I'm only trying to help" in the way you do. "I'm only trying to help" is actually a statement forged by the demons in hell to goad human beings into mass mutual self-destruction. After all, that is the devil's plan, and they are only trying to help.

I'm Too [FILL IN THE BLANK]

"I'm too old!" Is this what you are thinking over a contemplative cup of coffee as you consider whether to do something? Then allow me to say, "Ignore yourself."

You think you're too old? Too old for what? I have a friend who is ninety-five years old and still playing champion badminton in her age group. And no, posthumous participation is not allowed. They are all alive and well and whacking the heck out of the birdie.

Some say, "I'm too young." Are you really too young? If there are actual age restrictions that apply, think of the years you have to prepare! You can get in shape and take relevant classes in related studies to bolster your abilities and round out your skill sets. You may well end up significantly more qualified than the other candidates when the time comes, plus you will have demonstrated a continuity of commitment that the other candidates cannot turn back time to compete with.

If others say you're too old or too young, it doesn't matter. But if you say it, it does. So don't be too old or too young. If you must be "too" something in terms of age, be too young for doubt and too old for fear— no matter how old you are.

Some interpret a temporary state of being as the place they will be until God gives them a harp. They say things like, "I'm not good at … [math, English, technical stuff, dancing, singing, giving speeches, raising gerbils.]" They say, "I have no … [money, time, energy, computer skills, ability to fix things, patience, rhythm, hand-eye coordination, sense of direction, people skills.]" These things can all be adjusted, improved, corrected, and often mastered!

Many allow the word "but" to work as a deadbolt on their dream:

"I'd like to become an artist, BUT I'm partially color-blind."

"I'd like to be a doctor, BUT I don't have the money."

"I'd like to open an animal sanctuary, BUT I don't have any land."

"I'd like to make some home improvements, BUT I can't hammer a nail in straight and when I try to paint it looks like a roomful of squirrels dipped their tails in the paint can and ran amuck."

Try changing "BUT" to "AND," and your mind may popcorn up an inspiring array of solutions!

"I'd like to become an artist AND I'm partially color-blind." A career in black and white sketches opens before you!

"I'd like to be a doctor AND I don't have the money." Grants, scholarships, special programs, loans, and hard work become subjects of investigation!

"I'd like to open an animal sanctuary AND I don't have any land" leads you to a philanthropist who owns a field and is willing to fence it if you can build shelters and raise funds for food.

"I'd like to make some home improvements AND I can't hammer or paint" aims you toward the local home improvement store which has classes for that!

Are you perfecting the fine art of shooting yourself in the foot? Stopping before you start? Giving up before you even try? Are you indulging in fear instead of courting courageous, creative options to realize a dream or reach a goal? If you put in half the effort you invest in hobbling yourself into making progress, you would probably already be doing what you're busy convincing yourself you can't do.

After all, if you can toss dustsheets over your dreams like people do over furniture, close the blinds to the light of life, tiptoe out, and shut the door on possibilities, think what would happen if you reversed all those activities and opened up your life for new challenges! If you are strong enough to stop the progress of a human being created with almost infinite abilities, you are one powerful person! You convinced someone who can that they can't! Think what you could do if you started believing in yourself instead of belittling yourself. What could you do if you were on your own side? What if you put all your persuasion into encouraging yourself instead of convincing you to sideline yourself?

I challenge you that only a tiny spectrum of things you want to do is beyond you. You can achieve many things in full or achieve them enough to be happy. Think like the ninety-five-year-old badminton champ who, by the way, can still rock a little black dress. She is a member of the Optimists Club. Her name is Lee, and she is amazing. She does what she loves the way she can do it at whatever age she is. Be like Lee.

It's Always About Loving Her

D ue to I'm not sure what, more women than men seek advice. Men tend to avoid doctors who will tell them what to stop doing and marriage counselors who will tell them what to start doing.

Well, what would one expect from the sex that would prefer to drive until they run out of gas and then hitchhike in perpetuity, sleeping in boxes under bridges, rather than stop and ask for directions?

Men loathe admitting they don't know how to get from Point A to Point B, whereas women consider asking for help to be the shortest distance between those two points.

So, for all the men who will never ask but want to know how to avoid all the misunderstandings and arguments into which a relationship can disastrously descend, here is all you need to know:

Every fight you will ever have with a woman is really about whether or not you love her—no matter what you're fighting about.

Now isn't that simple? It would be. A man told me.

Let's say you are having a spirited discussion about taking out the trash. She asked if you would do it, you said yes but haven't quite gotten around to it and now instead of an argument about a sack of trash she is questioning your marriage vows. How did it come to this?!

Permit me to guide you through the maze of woman's reasoning that always leads to love.

She asked you to take out the trash, you said yes; however, you haven't taken it out yet, and this causes her to wonder if you really love her because if you loved her, you would care that it bothers her that she has cleaned the whole kitchen except for the bag of trash still slumped in the corner, and you would take care of the offending sack without forcing her to remind you to do it which always triggers the fight you are now having.

If you are arguing about going on vacation, you are arguing about loving her enough to understand she occasionally wants a vacation that offers mojitos instead of mosquitos, and blackjack instead of black bears and blisters. Unless you are arguing about loving her enough to know that her ideal vacation involves the Pyrenees Mountains and not poker tables.

If you are arguing about Valentine's Day, you are arguing about loving her enough to understand it Valentine-shames her when you do an eleventh-hour checkout line grab of sagging flowers and hardened chocolates rattling around in a heart-shaped cardboard box while Betty's husband Bob blinds her with a diamond tennis bracelet gleaming on velvet and Betty doesn't even play tennis!

Now you have the key. Far be it from me to give you the advice of using it! Here's a handy-dandy pop quiz so you can see for yourself if you've got it handled.

1. The backyard barbecue was great, but you are fussing about cleaning up the mess. What are you arguing about?
A. Who does what part of the clean-up?
B. Should you clean up now or kick back and take care of it tomorrow?

C. If you loved her, you'd understand that she can't just close the sliding glass doors on a cluttered, messy yard or get up in the morning to a kitchen splashed with salsa and crunchy with chips, and a sink towering with plates with food solidified on them.

2. The in-laws are coming! You're bickering about making the house presentable. What are you arguing about?

A. Who vacuums?

B. Who spit-shines the kitchen?

C. Who cleans the bathroom?

D. If you loved her, you'd know how much she wants her home to reflect her abilities to organize and keep her family safe and healthy in a clean, well-ordered home. Heaps of laundry, toothpaste blobs in the sink, and crumbs on the countertop tend to damage the image of efficiency—especially in her mother-in-law's eyes!

3. The kids are pushing boundaries and ignoring homework. You're disagreeing about their obviously doomed future. What are you arguing about?

A. The children's educational future?

B. The children's career future?

C. If you loved her, you would back her up. You're a team.

So! You got an "A" on the quiz, right? If you loved me, you'd say yes and affirm me as a writer.

KNOW HOW YOU'RE HARDWIRED

Have you ever seen Maslow's hierarchy of human needs? If one of your goals opposes any of Maslow's needs listed below, it will be an awful struggle to achieve it because you are working against your deepest drives.

1. Physiological (air, water, food, shelter, sleep, clothing)
2. Safety (security of body, employment, resources, family, health, property)
3. Belonging (friendship, family, sense of connection)
4. Esteem (respect, status, recognition)
5. Self-actualization (the desire to become the most that one can be)

Trying to lose weight is a good example of a goal triggering a struggle with these needs. As far as your body is concerned, dieting is a death threat!

Your body tells you it's hungry and you ignore it. What else can it infer other than there is no food? Red flags unfurl, and conservatory functions go into high gear. "Turn available food into fat so we can outlast the famine and be prepared for the next one," orders your body. The result? You regain the weight you lost plus a few pounds more. And there you are, opposing yourself and resisting your own efforts. You're yelling, "Put down that eclair and lose those pounds, darn it!" and your body is bellowing back, "But I need the calories!" If you were recorded at this moment you'd go viral and entertain the masses.

To get in shape, we cut back on fuel (food) while demanding our body increase its energy output in exercise. The body quite sensibly increases its demands for fuel (hunger pains and cravings) resulting in raids on the refrigerator as we despair that our will power is weak. The opposite is the problem—our will power is strong! And it is focused on survival. Our body thinks we are attempting suicide by broccoli. It's not a self-control issue— it's a self-preservation response!

Losing weight is a particularly complex goal because on one hand, it threatens the first and second hierarchical needs—food and bodily safety— and yet on the other hand it contributes to the well-being of needs four and five—esteem and self-actualization (becoming the best you can be). The battle pits you against yourself in a way that makes it extremely difficult to sustain a win at getting in shape. You are a formidable opponent! (For how to win at losing weight, I have added some advice at the end of this chapter. You're welcome!)

Let's say your new goal is to become better at public speaking. The only problem is that public speaking scares you spitless. You're not the only one. In some opinion polls, people are more afraid of public speaking than they are of dying! Why? Because …

Public speaking challenges ALL the needs on Maslow's list!

#1 Food, shelter, and clothing. These are hard to purchase when you're out of work, and poor presentation skills have torpedoed more than one career. If your brain freezes and refuses to thaw under fire, your ability to contribute to team meetings will suffer. A conference table ringed in corporate representatives can be just as intimidating as an auditorium packed with conference attendees. You're laboring under extreme performance pressure and wishing you were anywhere else.

#2 Safety. It isn't a "safe" feeling when you stand up in front of a roomful of people with the mission of holding their attention as you entertain, educate, and motivate them. You're very much outnumbered, and if they don't like you, they can throw things at you. It isn't a warm and cozy feeling to stand up there with only a lonely lectern between you and the jeering masses!

#3 Belonging. If you're a glib public speaker, you feel right at home. If not, you have never been more alone in your life. You are not part of the group; you are the "other."

#4 Esteem. Your audience can ask questions that you flounder in answering. They can turn in Human Resource reviews of your performance that do not bode well for promotion. Public speaking is an opportunity for respect, status, and recognition, and also an opportunity to lessen those three elements of success. Your esteem can be positively massacred. Why do you think they call it "bombing" when you fail in front of a crowd? You are reduced to human rubble.

#5 Self-actualization. If your presentation doesn't go so well, it can seriously hamper your belief that you have the ability to become all you can be.

Gee, I wonder why people are so afraid of public speaking?

Even simple things can put you into opposition to yourself in meeting one of Maslow's needs. Being social energizes extroverts. For introverts, meeting and mixing with others is stressful—an excruciating experience that makes their smile feel like stretched rubber and turns their brain into a blank screen with a blinking curser awaiting words to contribute to the conversation. They are struggling with safety, belonging, and self-esteem.

So, if your home is your quiet castle, and a movie or a good book is your way to relax and recharge, now you know why it's so hard to mingle. You want to slip out the back door, start your engine as quietly as possible, and drive away. The description is detailed because I have done it many times.

The point of this chapter is to help you be aware when you are in opposition to yourself. It may not be true that you are a lazy, unmotivated, self-indulgent sloth. We are too hard on ourselves much of the time. Why wait for others to judge and condemn us when we can do it ourselves and get it over with? Instead, look a little deeper.

Imagine you have written the next great American novel and your challenge is to get it from your PC to the world. Writing was the easy part, as it turns out. You freeze and won't research how to publish. You panic and over-research how to publish. But you won't actually publish! We call it fear of failure. If you don't try, you will not fail. You'd rather hear silence than the word "no." Also, let us be frank, it's a heck of a lot of hard work to put in and end up with a drawer of rejection letters. Why not just let it be a pleasantly affirming possibility? Look at you! You wrote a book! Let's stop with a happy ending.

Keeping fear of failure in mind, take another look at Maslow's needs and consider which one(s) you might be coming up against:

1. Physiological (air, water, food, shelter, sleep, clothing)
2. Safety (security of body, employment, resources family, health, property)
3. Belonging (friendship, family, sense of connection)
4. Esteem (respect, status, recognition)
5. Self-actualization (the desire to become the most that one can be)

What did you come up with? I think it's numbers three through five. Will you belong to the published few or the rejected many? Will you enjoy respect, status, and recognition, or their opposites? Will you actually become the writer you know you are or will rejections make that self-concept appear ridiculous?

Can you see how you'd rather not find out? On the other hand …

Think of it as crossing the finish line. Imagine you're at the track and you've bet on Sir Winsalot. Your horse thunders down the track in a three-nose tie for first place and … digs in his front hooves in a dust-raising, jockey-hurling dead stop. The other two horses blaze across the finish line. What?? You tear your ticket into ribbons and stomp off. Stupid horse! But wait … in this analogy, you are the horse. Don't stop short of your own finish line. Satisfy the needs listed in numbers three, four, and five.

Give yourself the opportunity to be in the good company of writers who honor their work.

Give yourself the respect, status, and recognition of finishing the race.

Give yourself the option of becoming all you can be.

Then you will no longer be in opposition to yourself—you will be your own champion.

* As I promised, here are my suggestions for getting in better shape without losing a battle against your own body. They all work to keep you thinking and focusing in ways that put your health goals in sync with your hard-wired needs.

Focus on eating MORE food, not less.

Eat a bunny-food salad AND a cup of soup before lunch and dinner. Finish with a small plate of sliced fruit. It works. Make it a mantra: I have to eat more food! It will neutralize your body's survival-triggered fear of deprivation. It will amp up your nutrition and decrease junk food cravings. Have a plastic food storage container at the table and put all the uneaten food in it. This removes the dictum of finishing your food even though you're full. Think, *Wow! I get to eat an extra time today! This can be an afternoon snack!*

Focus on eating rather than not eating.

Think nutrition and variety. Think flavor! (I use fresh diced salsa as a vegetable dip.) Add good things to your food life. Let the low-nutrition and junk foods be like falling leaves as the buds of new leaves gently push them out of the way.

Focus on moving your body gently.

Gently build a foundation of strength, and your body will go from strength to strength. It's fun to realize the weights feel light! It's so cool the day you feel like putting a little more speed on the treadmill! Of course, if you prefer soreness and fatigue, give your body an overnight demand to get out of the easy chair, go to the gym, and do thirty minutes of heart-pounding cardio followed by free-weights and varied with killer classes where you imperil your existence by trying to keep up with the instructor and the class. You might as well strap your body to a train engine and ask it to pull. It's so unkind to you!

Remember, if you abruptly ask a body in stasis to be a body in motion, it will think you must be in danger of intergalactic assault and do its very best to strain every muscle, ligament, and joint to its utmost to cooperate and get to safety. But after that, of course, it requires a lot of care and rest which you cannot give it because you are on an exercise schedule that would cripple a carthorse. This unkindness will make your body resist a repetition of these horrendous events, and you will find yourself opposing yourself. Again.

Make one SMALL change at a time.

Small victories win great wars. Build slowly on each success. Let your body adapt. Build gently and consistently, and let the benefits add up: strength, easier movement, the pleasant sensation of energy.

Alter your "set weight" ten pounds at a time.

Your body has a set weight. Whether it's nine pounds or nine hundred pounds, it will defend that set weight not because the weight itself is healthy but because it perceives maintaining the status quo as beneficial. Lower it ten pounds at a time, which is about one clothing size. Allow the new weight to become your new set weight so your body will work to support your next weight loss. If you push for more weight loss immediately, your body will fight to return to the former set weight.

LET'S (NOT) TALK POLITICS

The American people are an affable, friendly sort! They can agree, or agree to disagree, on many subjects. That's why there are two main political parties! Isn't it? We can have different points of view yet live in the same country. It's worked pretty well so far, even surviving a civil war.

In fact, we are such nice guys that there are only two things we can't agree on. Who the President should be and who God is.

The French say that politeness is the oil of society. It helps us function together smoothly. In America, polite silence was the key to getting on about politics and religion. Our grandparents didn't discuss them at parties, our parents didn't discuss them at parties. Then social media slithered onto the scene like the snake in the Garden of Eden and now we DO discuss them. Everywhere. All the time. Oh dear. Politics can have Uncle Joe and Uncle Pete throttling each other on the picnic table at the family reunion.

Politics is a singularly disinterested entity. It is equally willing to serve the cause of good or evil. Politics is not a person, but it combines the force of many people united for whatever their cause may be. It is defined through thought but once decided is not appreciative of challenges or further thought. It is the product of discussion, but once decided is oddly closed to further discussion.

Religion is completely universal and completely private at the same time. Our interior journey to our decision is uniquely our own.

Both politics and religion have the curious effect, once decided, of becoming bedrock to our being. We actually don't want to discuss them. We want to convert others to ours. A political position and a religious belief have more in common than is comfortable to consider. They are the decisions of human beings who may agree on little other than the inevitability of death and taxes.

Perhaps the power of mankind to govern themselves and to be or not be governed by their God is something too deep for the shallow waters of social media.

My advice? Respect each other. We can completely disagree with each other, even work against each other if we are convinced we must, and still respect our human right to choose our government on earth and in heaven.

LOVE OVERFLOW

L ove is made to pour into us and out of us. It's like water. Water is lovely stuff but if a pond or lake doesn't have water flowing in and water flowing out, what do we call it? Stagnant. We are made to give and receive love.

When my first husband died, I felt like I was hemorrhaging love with no one to receive it. I was still in love with him even though he was gone and our connection was severed, and the love just poured out into the universe like some ectoplasmic thing.

I learned a secret from this experience. The song lyrics are true. "What the world needs now is love, sweet love, it's the only thing that there's just too little of." There is joy, purpose, and comfort in letting your love overflow into the world around you to those who need it. Look for who, and even what, needs love, and give it yours. You can love people, a good cause, or a garden.

Giving your love this way has another benefit as well. A loving person is very attractive. If you want a mate to love, don't cocoon and wait for them. Don't exhaust yourself in search of them. Go into your world as it is and give the love that is yours to give. Then someday you will fall in love again, and there will be a stream that blends with yours into a new river.

That is the way of it.

Not That You Like Them or Anything

We can be slightly self-deceptive about relationships.

Love is blind in more ways than one. It can make us blind to ourselves. We find reasons to be wherever they are. We remember everything they say. Yet we think we are so subtle! We think we can sneak up on the object of our affection without their having a clue. Gwen Cooper, author of "Homer's Odyssey," an amazing book about her blind cat, wrote of his stealthy efforts to sneak up on her two other cats. He made every effort to be silent, not realizing that they could see him as he crept toward them! We are exactly like that when we're in love. We think the object of our affection won't notice that wherever they go, there we are!

We develop a severe case of "mentionitis," bringing their name into every conversation by routes so complex few can follow them. The football team wins, and you shout over the celebratory tumult at the local sports bar that Henry was a high school quarterback. Not that you like him or anything.

We do special things for them as if it is no big deal. One girl arranged for a "happy birthday" message for a man she recently met to be added to the glittering ball dropped in the city's downtown New Year's Eve celebration. He reacted by being immensely discomfited by her over-reach. She protested that it was just a "friendly" thing to do and didn't convey any message of interest in him. Um … okay. Another girl baked frog-shaped cookies for a boss she liked. Oh tra-la-la, it was nothing, really nothing!

Blow a loud whistle and call a halt to over-reaching or, in fact, reaching out at all. Let someone reach out to you instead.

And if no one is reaching for you right now, my advice is not to try to become a presence in someone ELSE'S life but to become a presence in your OWN life! That is attractive. So be the interesting, fun, happy, curious, creative, active person you actually are. Fully occupy your life and live it to the full. Instead of being the moon looking for light to reflect, become the sun, shine on your universe, and notice all the planets orbiting into your life.

OTHER PEOPLE'S CHILDREN

Ever watched as kids ignore their parents' protests and run amuck with no consequences other than, "If I have to tell you one more time ...!"? Honestly! Other peoples' children!

I am a stern disciplinarian—of other people's children. With my own children, I am a bowl of mush.

Full disclosure—my children are very furry. One was a willful little calico with velvety fur who loved us and went on walks with me through the forest. I would have taken a bullet for her. One day she was getting into everything, and my husband's generous store of patience was waning. "Make her get off the table!" he said. So I turned to her, and in a voice that distinctly said, "Oh you are the darlin'est little thing!" the words I said were, "Oh you bad little cat!" My husband remarked ruefully, "Oh, that'll do it." I just couldn't be stern with her. I loved her too much. I didn't want to see her green eyes widen in alarm and watch her scoot away from me.

I treasure the love of my kitties ... the dreamy look they get as they gaze at me affectionately when I cradle them. The way they believe me when I tell them it's going to be all right at the vet's office. I don't mind if they stand at the door and meow to get out when it's too late at night to let them go. I don't scold them. I pick them up, love on them, and offer them kitty treats to distract them.

I start out defending my plate of food and end up caving in and offering them bites. If they want to sleep curled around my head, I let them. I buy them whatever kind of food they love. I put catnip spray on their scratching post. I see to it that they have a safe place to run to if something scares them. If my cat is curled up in kitty bliss on my desk chair, I take my laptop over to my recliner and work there instead. If he walks across my keyboard, I patiently erase the letters he types. If he sniffs my coffee with cream in it, I pour him some cream of his own.

I want him to be happy and know he is loved. Making him happy makes me happy. Love is like that.

Other people's children, however, are a different matter. In the echoing walls of the grocery store, the ear-splitting shrieks of two children made conversation impossible except between their parents. As the two little ones playfully screamed at full volume, their parents discussed what meat they should select for dinner. They were as deaf to their children's scream-athon as they were blind to the rolling eyes and pained flinching of the nearby shoppers. *What? Oh, that's my kitty. He's fine, he's just meowing to be let out. He'll stop eventually. Just ignore him.*

Why is it that children's rooms look like a rummage sale and the living room looks like a daycare center? I'll never understand why parents just let their kids take over the whole house! *Oh, those are his toys. He leaves them everywhere. Sorry for the hairy chair. Here, let me toss a throw blanket over it so you can sit.*

And I wish they would train their children to let the adults have an uninterrupted conversation. Some of my friends just let their kids…

Oh look! He likes you! Oops! Sorry! That head-butt means he wants to be petted. Sorry he did it just as you were trying to drink your coffee! Let me get you a napkin.

My advice? Smile, and say nothing. Love is just like that.

REMEMBER WE ARE PRIMEVAL

The classic relationship film, *When Harry Met Sally*, was inspired by the post-divorce experience of director, Rob Reiner. He wanted to be able to have consensual sex with women friends without serious romantic involvement but found that sex ruined the friendships. "I'm not saying it meant nothing, but why does it have to mean everything?" asks a desperate Harry. "Because it does," cries a frustrated Sally.

I have a deeper answer for Harry—because women have the babies.

Men are sexual goldfish. Goldfish are said to have a memory of two seconds. Men are in a dead heat with this memory limit when it comes to recalling physical encounters. "I'll call you," is the last thing they can remember saying; they just can't quite recall who they said it to.

Women, on the other hand, after a sexual encounter, may be left with a human being in their womb. Sexual pleasure is a nice perk to a very serious process essential to the continuation of life on this planet. Women know this on a primeval level. Men know, "Oh goody, sex!"

To generalize, for men sex is an appetite to be satisfied. You're hungry, you eat, you're done. Actor Paul Newman, an iconic sex symbol, was known for his faithfulness to his wife. Most unfortunately, he acknowledged this as follows, "Why would I go out for hamburger when I have steak at home?"

(And now you know why actors have scripts.) For men, it can be this way. For women, it simply can't. They have to take the possible consequence into consideration. Why just the women? Well, ideally, the potential father should be taking it into consideration too. But do they? Why not? Because women have the baby. For the men, we are back to, "Oh goody!"

My point is that women are aware of the serious side of sex. If they forget, they can count on a monthly reminder that their role is far different than a man's. A girlfriend of mine once referred to her period as "clearing out an empty house." The possibility of an occupant is never far from our primeval female mind.

Now we come to it. This is why women are more romantic, more relationship-oriented, more commitment inclined, and yes—more marriage-minded—than men. It makes perfect sense. All the legal advancements, societal evolvement, and pharmaceutical progression put together still cannot overrule thousands of years embedded in our core. And since we are two weeks of food and five showers away from uncivilized behavior and one nuclear strike away from an unrecognizably primitive environment, perhaps it's best they can't.

When the morning after a romantic night dawns, women are hoping that men will call not because they are clingy or marriage-crazy, but because an ancient connection with our reproductive system wisely wants connection that will provide future provision and protection. What? Provision and protection? What's next? Bringing back chaperones? Women work, for heaven's sake! They can support themselves and raise a family on their own. They are doing it all over the nation! Again, remember we are primeval. And consider what I noticed in a genealogy book.

In its pages, I found an interesting pattern. Couples had truckloads of children! Families of sixteen children were common. Many had twenty-two children or more. Then the wife would pass away (wouldn't you?) and the man would remarry and have twenty-two more children! Childhood diseases caused so many deaths that the children who survived were often relatively few, so this marriage/reproductive two-step helped ensure the continuation of the species. When a woman is the mother of eighteen children and carrying a nineteenth, she is sane to want an environment where her family is protected and provided for. A good marriage provides that.

This former two-marriage pattern was also in sync with the fact that a woman's childbearing years end in middle age because her ova deteriorate in quality as she ages. A man's sperm do not. He can make babies all his life. Women wear out from childbearing and die. The men, obviously, manage to survive pacing the floor and chain-smoking cigars during the delivery of their progeny, and live to remarry.

This marriage/remarriage continuum also explains something else. When a mature man marries a younger woman—let's say a man in his early fifties marries a woman in her thirties—the twenty-year age difference may raise a few eyebrows and prompt a few rib-jabbing jokes, but when a mature woman marries a younger man, those eyebrows arch a little higher. We label these older women as if they were on display in a sexual zoo. A woman in her thirties who simply prefers younger men is called a puma. But a woman in her forties or fifties who seeks out men at least ten years younger and often half her age is branded a cougar—an aggressive huntress. What do we call an older man who dates younger women? Lucky.

I suspect that underneath the puma/cougar labels, an ancient dynamic is at work. An older man can create a second family with a younger woman. It has dignified societal undertones. It has honor and purpose. An older woman, relieved by menopause of pregnancy issues, who prefers young men is perceived by some as starkly guilty of pursuing hot sex with no redeeming societal value whatever. Not that they are judging.

The primeval core recognizes the older man/younger woman pairing. It views a non-fertile woman culling the herd of virile males as simply sapping the population.

The transformation of women in society has made rapid advances. In some formal marriage ceremonies, the walking of the bride down the aisle by her father and his handing her off to the groom originally symbolized something that does not exist today—the transference from her father's house to her husband's. In times past, a woman could not take responsibility for herself as we do today. They could not vote, own property, control their own banking, or have a career. They were dependent on their husband. If they never married and their father passed away, they would move to the home of the nearest male relative.

Can you even imagine a world where you did not have the option of living an independent life on your own terms? Actually, you can imagine it, at your core. Today, birth control is available, women control their own lives, and emergency help is three digits away. Protection and provision are covered. Yet deep within us, the desire for marriage and stability, honor and commitment is born of dangerous times just a blink ago in history.

And that is why you want him to call the next day. That is why you may be more commitment-comfortable and more marriage-minded than you care to admit. You can't override the input of eons. And you might not even want to. Just as there is much to be said for financial independence and the sexual freedom bestowed by birth control, there is much to be said for a life partner who loves you and helps care for his family. Perhaps Mother Nature isn't quite as old-fashioned as she may seem. Maybe she's just practical. Women are like that. We have to be. Because babies.

ROSE-COLORED GLASSES

We marry the most wonderful man in the world! We melt at the sound of his voice. He is all things wonderful, and we love him madly! A few years later, he is a sock-dropping sports addict who never listens.

Have you ever read your journal entries during your dating days? Mine are positively lyrical with adoration of my husband. He was a man among men, so gentle and kind, so considerate and loving. He still is. But there was an interim where the inevitable differences between men and women added a few thorns to the roses of love. One day, though, I realized he hadn't changed—I had changed. I was taking the good things for granted. My focus had changed to the things that bothered me.

Couples still in love after many decades ignore more things than they choose to notice. And they choose to notice the things that are good.

It would be better if we leave the rose-colored glasses in their case during courtship so we can see clearly and then put them on after marriage so we can see kindly, but we tend to do it the other way around.

Leave the rose-colored glasses off during courtship so you can avoid marrying the wrong person.

Are you constantly explaining or excusing your partner's behavior? He stands you up because he is a focused genius and gets lost in his work! He is short-tempered for the same reason. He doesn't like big, friendly family gatherings … for the same reason. He's a quirky, brilliant lone wolf! No, he's not a barely functional sociopath or a self-centered bastard or a man not remotely qualified to be a husband much less a father! Your friends and family just don't understand him.

Oh yes, they do! Take off the darn glasses! Take a long, justification-free look at the one you will have to adjust to, explain, and forgive for the rest of your life.

Put them on after marriage to avoid losing the right person.

Co-habitation of two sexes who struggle to understand each other can create conflicts which may cause you to think you made a mistake. You may have, but you probably didn't. If all you can see is the flaws you are obsessing about, it may be because you are focusing on them. Focus magnifies things. When you focus on the negative, of course it's all you see! Once upon a time, their good points were all consuming. Cultivate the habit of thinking of all the wonderful things they are and you may find that the stuff which used to bug you just tends to reveal them as human. As I once said to my husband, "Sweetheart, you don't have faults—you have character traits!"

Consider this ancient advice: Remember your first love. (If that sounds familiar, it's because it is similar to what Jesus said to a church in Revelations 2:4.) Read your journals from your courtship days. Look at your first photo albums. Did you write your friends about him in the beginning? Ask if they still have the letters. I recently sent an old friend the cards and letters she sent me during her courtship days, each one a soaring kite of happiness! Treasures, every one of them.

The time to see clearly is before you marry. The time to see through a softened lens is after you marry. They may never be perfect, but if you married the right person, you will find they are perfect for you. Focus on seeing them in terms of what they are, instead of focusing on what they are not. It really works!

SIGNAGE

As I drive, I often marvel that companies pay for billboards that tell you nothing about who they are or what they do.

I further marvel that those companies paid another company big bucks to come up with the nothing that is on the billboard! Hey—can I work for you guys? I can write nothing for money too!

Here is what I mean. A big billboard splashed with happy people and the anacronym PDOW* is supposed to mean something to you. Is it a hotel? Golf course? College campus? Bank? Hospital?

I looked up one of these mystery-letters billboards and discovered it was a credit union. Oh. But even knowing that, what am I supposed to do about it? I assume they want me to join, but no contact info was on the billboard.

Sometimes the smiling people on the billboard are accompanied by a generic phrase. "Because life can be wonderful!"* I agree. And *who* are you? At the risk of driving off the road into the billboard, I squint and see a website. BestDays.com.* Is it a retirement community? A senior citizen multi-vitamin? A vacation destination?

I know you probably don't have a billboard of your own, but you can take these thoughts into consideration when you have events to post around town.

Here is some advice on how to make people stop, look, and pay attention to your sign.

Keep in mind that people have about *three seconds* to read your notice on a telephone pole or fence if they are driving by.

Signs and notices are everywhere. Your sign should draw their attention even before they know what it is. Color works, and so does an imaginative font (that is easy to read). Photos draw more attention than words. Use a cast photo on a theater poster, for instance.

First, make a headline that grabs them.

Second, be clear what action you want them to take. List the information in the order they will need to do what you want them to do—drive by the yard sale, keep an eye out for your missing fur-baby, etc.

Don't splatter graphic images here, there, and everywhere. Allow their eyes to focus on your headline message. Don't use a lot of small print. Most people won't read it.

Headline: LOST CAT

[Large print] Area where they went missing.

(If the poster reader lives in that area, now they are paying attention.)

COLOR photo (even if your pet is white, gray, or black) with their name.

[Large print] The phone number to call and any reward offered.

Then add all the details, such as medication needs, the color of their collar, etc. One caution: Putting the date they went missing in large print may stop some people from looking for them as time goes by. Consider putting that date in the details portion of your sign.

Headline: GARAGE SALE

Consider adding a motivating adjective: MOVING SALE, NEIGHBORHOOD GARAGE SALE, CUL-DE-SAC GARAGE SALE.

[Large print] Location

[Large print] When

Everything else can be in smaller print.

How to Stand Out on a Notice Board

You want them to notice YOUR poster if it's among many others. Try angling it a little. Everyone else's will be vertical. Angle a poster and it makes everybody look. It's like a picture on the wall—even if people are driven to look at it only because they are suddenly gripped with a desire to straighten it, at least they are focusing on it!

Buy (or make) "lookit me!" arrow stickers and use them to point at the headline of your poster. Color printing can be pricey so add your own color around the headline or edges.

Will the sun be hitting it? Sprinkle sparkles on it!

Rainy weather? Invest in plastic covers.

As you post, take scotch tape and thumb tacks with you to accommodate wherever you put them up. Make a note of where you put your posters and drive by them now and then to see if yours is still easy to see and in good condition. Take more posters with you to replace yours if necessary.

And if you're really a wonderful person, when the event is over, drive around and take them down.

Doesn't a teensy negative thought go through your mind when you see tacky, out-of-date, weather-beaten posters? Don't let one of them be yours.

*I made it up. Don't do a search for it.

THE BALL AND THE BEE

It's confusing. We want something to happen in our lives and pursue it as best we can, but we just can't make it happen! On the other hand, we bemoan the repetition of certain experiences we would rather not have and yet they arrive as steadily as waves on the shore.

Upon what mountaintop must we meditate for how long to understand what the heck is going on? I don't know. Personally, I am afraid of heights. But I did one day discover an applicable principal lurking in my experiences with either a ball or a bee in a pool.

Have you ever been happily splashing and floating in a cool swimming pool on a hot day and then noticed a bee in the water near you? I prefer distance between myself and anything that stings, so I would try to swim away or paddle my plastic raft away (so I could get out and rescue the bee, actually), and every time the bee would be sucked along in my wake and end up even closer! So, I would stay still and swoosh water at it to make it move away, but that backfired, too! The bee seemed to rise to the top of the little waves I made and "surf" down them to be even closer to me!

Then I would have the exact reverse experience with a ball in the water. I wanted the ball to come closer so I would swim or paddle toward it, and my forward motion made little waves that pushed it away. So, I would make swooshing motions toward me, trying to coax the ball within reach.

Nothing doing. As I made the downward motions toward myself, I created little waves that rose and broke away from me, taking the ball with them!

I made some conclusions from these puzzling experiences. Trying to draw something to you may generate currents that push it away from you. Trying to push something away from you may generate currents that draw it toward you.

We call it "trying too hard." We seem to have an innate sense about it. When someone "tries too hard" to make friends with us, we resist. Instead of a natural camaraderie developing, they push to spend time together, perhaps call too often, share too much too fast, or persist in buying us small gifts. If we try too hard to push things away—from excess pounds to an insistent suitor—they try harder to stay or come closer.

The alternative is "being." It works in two ways. If you "are" something, you will attract it. If you are friendly, you will attract friends. They will gravitate to you without you calling, texting, or otherwise pulling them in. And if you "are" something, things that are *not* like you will drift away without your "trying to" make them go away. For instance, if you are a healthy eater, cravings subside.

It is very complex, it is a spiritual principal, it is a creative principal. There is authenticity and balance in "being." It comes across as strength. It inspires trust. We want to work with, be friends with, hire, marry, and just in general hang around with authentic, balanced people. They don't smell of insecurity, need, uncertainty, or fear.

Balanced beings give us room to take a step closer, so we do. One real estate agent learned that the best way to invite prospective buyers into an open house was to open the door wide as she walked backward into the house, which drew people in.

If you want others to step forward, step back a little. Literally or figuratively. Give them room to make up their mind, experience attraction, and move toward your life.

Limit your "reaches." Reaches can be subconscious ways to put others in social debt.

If you are always the one who gets in touch, cut back. Let space develop between you to give them room to reach out. If you are always the one who provides or pays, stop. Give them room to honor you in that way. Create a space where their options can dwell. Let them have their choice, their power, their preference.

When peace replaces struggle, you would be amazed at what good things float gently into your reach. Like a beach ball.

THE BEST ADVICE FOR EVERYONE EVERYWHERE

Whether you believe in a next life or not, we can probably agree that living your best life is important, rewarding, and fulfilling. Do a search for "live your best life" books and see how many books are written on the subject! And if that's not enough, I appeal to Oprah! It is the theme for her magazine.

Jesus prefaced his earthly ministry with a forty-day fast in solitude (Matthew 4:1-11). At the end of it, he was famished, and Satan showed up with three temptations. These temptations are the same three he offers everyone. Apparently, they work because there is no fourth. I thought you might like to know what they are so you don't fall for any of them.

The three temptations are: to save your life (at the expense of losing your soul), to risk your life, and to waste your life.

Satan started all three temptations with, "If you are the son of God …" He knew perfectly well who Jesus was! Why did he do that? Because there are two dares responsible for most of the follies committed by humankind. "What's the matter—are you chicken?" and "Prove it!" Apparently, we are total suckers for both. Satan was hoping Jesus would be too. But he wasn't.

Don't Lose Your Life

The first temptation is: "If you are the son of God, command these stones to turn into bread."

Jesus replied, "It is written, 'Man shall not live by bread alone but by every word that proceeds from the mouth of God.'"

Satan tempted Him when His physical body was at its weakest. If Jesus had caved in to his hunger and used His miraculous power to turn the stones into bread, He would have been valuing his physical body over His spiritual destiny. The Spirit led Him into the wilderness for a time of consecration and preparation. A loaf of bread was nothing in comparison. Satan tempted Him to jump the gun and get what His body was yearning for. It's a very effective temptation. It leads people into adultery all the time.

Don't Risk Your Life

The second temptation is: "If you are the son of God, throw yourself down [from the highest point of the temple] for it is written: 'He will command his angels concerning you, and they will lift you up in their hands, so that you will not strike your foot against a stone.'"

Jesus replied, "It is also written: 'Do not put the Lord your God to the test.'"

There are teenagers eating detergent soap pods which could kill them just to take a dare and prove they are brave. They are counting on being ten feet tall and bulletproof. They are neither. There is nothing brave about doing something pointlessly stupid, but when our ego is mocked, our courage questioned, our group loyalty put to the test, it is amazing how we will risk our lives. What about the risk of drunk driving? Somewhere in these risks is an assumption we may not even know we are making. We think we won't actually die from our own foolishness. We may be wrong.

Don't Waste Your Life

The third temptation is: "Again, the devil took him to a very high mountain and showed him all the kingdoms of the world and their splendor. 'All this I will give you,' he said, 'if you will bow down and worship me.'"

Jesus replied, "Away from me, Satan! For it is written: 'Worship the Lord your God and serve him only.'"

This is a trick temptation. All the kingdoms of the world already belonged to Jesus. Sometimes Satan tempts us with something God has already promised to give us as we walk with Him. If we turn from the paths of righteousness and swerve over a lane or two to obtain it wrongfully, Satan succeeds. Don't let him. And if we let "things" become the desire of our heart to the point where we dedicate our lives to achieving them, we have wasted our life because Jesus said, "It is the Father's good pleasure to GIVE YOU the kingdom." Don't let Satan trick you into giving up what God will give you freely and permanently so he can "give" it to you temporarily at the price of your soul. Truly, nothing and no one on Earth is worth it. Or, as Jesus said in Matthew 16:26, "What good will it be for someone to gain the whole world, yet forfeit their soul?"

You see, it isn't about the bread, the foolish or exciting risk, or the power, fame, or glory. It's about the human soul. Your soul. Nothing is more important or precious. It is worth more than anything this life can offer. Your soul was worth the life of Jesus to redeem it, which He loved you enough to do. Don't risk it, waste it, or lose it by valuing anything else more.

THE DARK SIDE OF SCHOOL

I will begin with the advice. Help your child find their tribe. I think many parents send their children off to school by telling them to have a good day and then welcome them home asking how their day was. We ask about homework and try our hardest to get them to admit it if they have a special project that is due the next day.

We concern ourselves with the hours they spend in the classroom. But it's the hours spent out of the classroom at school that can be the despair of a child's life.

For the shy ones, the sensitive ones, the unusual ones, recess and lunch may be daily humiliations that expose their outsiderness, their otherness. When teams are chosen, they are the last ones standing as a team captain shrugs and signals them to join. Eating in miserable isolation or hiding out in the bathroom or library are the lunchtime fates of the lonely. I remember one well-meaning teacher who saw me eating lunch in the girls' bathroom and insisted with a sprightly smile that I "go out in the sunshine." She briskly walked away thinking she had done her good deed for the day. I resorted to the library instead where the only food I could smuggle in was chips.

ADVICE

Your child may be friendless, and you may never notice. If your child walks to and from school alone, it may never occur to you that other children in their school also live in your neighborhood but are walking together in closed groups. It may never occur to you that when your child is out of school, they are home. Where are their friends? The knock on the door asking if they can come out and play? When holidays come, are they invited to parties? Or are they only invited to events when the whole classroom is invited?

Participating in officially organized activities is different than having friends. Just as an adult can join a reading club yet never go for coffee with anyone in the club, it is quite possible for a child to be socially busy yet friendless. If they didn't show up, no one would care. They are so very alone at the time of their lives when friends mean everything.

If enrolling them into social activities isn't the cure for their friendlessness, what is? The odds of your child finding a tribe increase when they hang out with others who share their interests or abilities. As a child, I loved to read. I was drawn to theater. I played the guitar by ear and liked to sing. What would you have done with me? You would have involved me in things I loved. Pushing me out the door into summer sports would have had me benched all season. I was terrible at sports. Enrolling me in summer school would have extended the hollow social experience of the school year.

Be careful what you cheerfully suggest to your child. I was terrified of school dances during middle school. Taller than most of the boys and without friends among the girls, I stood there like a giant stalk of corn in a field of flowers, and I suffered. My mother's non-helpful advice was to ask the boys to dance. I tried it one time. I actually got up my nerve and crossed "the great divide" of the dance floor between the girls grouped on one side and the boys huddled on the other. The first boy said no, so the second boy hastily said no as well. I didn't know what to do! I clumsily asked a few other boys standing around me, and when they all literally backed away, I

~ 133 ~

was stranded on the boys' side of the room with nothing to do but walk to the back wall and escape out the exit.

Following your bright idea to, "Just go sit at their table and say hello!" at lunchtime will subject your child to incredulous looks and giggles. Asking boys to dance will be an experience they will write about in a book someday.

In high school, I eventually met two fellow fans of the Beatles. We bonded and even attended one of their concerts where we couldn't hear them over the screaming, but we could glimpse them in our binoculars. Those days of having someone to hang out with at lunch were the most socially relaxed days of my high school experience.

It doesn't take a lot of friends—just one or two. They are like your child in some way. There is common ground. They are smart, funny, sweet, and will make life better. Some children have one friend. One friend is enough. If they eventually move on from one best friend to a new best friend, that will do as well. Not everyone is an extrovert, after all.

You can also tell your child that conformity tends to be the price of success in a school environment, but the world is waiting for outstanding individuals. Tell them that even though now they would give their kingdom to be ordinary, they are one of the amazing ones. And there are others out there just like them. The amazing ones who one day will find their element, their wings, their stride. And you are so proud one of them is your child.

P.S. If you are the parent of an out-going child with lots of friends, they are probably one of the compassionate few who will befriend someone less socially fortunate. Encourage them to use their social strengths for good. Tell them how wonderful they are to care about others as much as they do.

THE GAMES MEN PLAY

Not all men play games. I have known many wonderful, honorable men in my life. Men of my father's generation and men of my own. But who needs advice on how to handle honorable men? We need to know how to spot the other kind.

We've come a long way from the days of formal courtship when a chaperone was always present. We progressed to "dating" and whizzed right along to "hanging," and whether or not that is progress I will leave it to you to judge. But I think one thing endured through all these social metamorphoses. Women are romantic about romance. This makes them vulnerable to men who are sexually predatory and willing to manipulate a woman into intimacy.

Perhaps romance is Mother Nature's way of blinding us to the lifetime of child-bearing that awaits us if She has her way. But our tendency to romanticize makes it hard for us to believe that a good-looking man can ask us out and be totally dreamy and still be pond scum.

You don't have to be cynical or bitter to be a realist. You can just be someone who knows there are sexual sharks trolling the waters of life looking for gullible victims. Here are some terrible but true stories that prove they do indeed exist:

One man told me that making strong forward moves with a woman and being ultra-romantic and intimate at first, then suddenly doing a huge pullback, creates a powerful emotional undertow that sucks her in and makes her desperate to be with him. He said it works every time. (This suggests a possibility that if a man sweeps you off your feet and then stops calling, he is either genuinely gone or manipulating you into shameless antics to regain his attention. Either way, consider yourself fortunate—not abandoned.)

Another man told me that the way to attract a hard-to-get woman at a night club was to ask her friends to dance instead of asking her. Ultimately, she would make a move, and because it was her idea, she would regard him as a conquest when actually it was the other way around. He took it further. If there was a very sought-after woman who frequented a bar or club, he would deliberately sleep with the other women who went there so the word would get around that he was a good lover. Eventually the hard-to-get woman would approach him because she was curious and couldn't figure out why he was sleeping with everyone but her! If he had approached her first, he would have been like all the other men, and she might have rejected him. This same man said that if he tried to sleep with a woman and she said no, he would circle back into her life, like a shark, about a year later and try again because "no" never meant "no," it just meant not today. The women would think he liked them enough to come back to them. He was actually just hoping for a vulnerable moment.

Going back in time to a more sexually conservative generation, my dad told me about one of his friends who was very good-looking and very charming. He regularly seduced women by seeming to make a woman's romantic dreams of a whirlwind courtship come true. In one evening, he would chat her up, charm her completely, pretend to fall in love with her, propose marriage and she would say an ecstatic yes, and they would have a magical night. Normally she would never have gone to bed on the first date or considered doing a one-night stand. Which is what it would turn out to be.

Seducers mimic the behavior of men in love. They do it so well, their imitation can be more believable than the real thing. They are like cubic zirconia that sparkle more brightly than true diamonds. They often have a more sensitive understanding of women than honorable men do. They seem to know the secrets of your heart and how to make a woman feel adored.

Seducers know how to listen and respond in a way that makes a woman feel truly heard and understood. It is called "the art of seduction" for a reason. It's a skill. We call them smooth talkers because they are!

Of course, while they are hanging on your every word and making you feel heard and understood and precious for the first time in your life, they are mentally ticking off the days until your tree finally falls in their forest, so to speak. Or they are adding up how many dinners and romantic walks they have to rack up before you succumb to their charm. They might as well be sitting there with a calculator and a calendar.

How can you tell the difference between noble men and scoundrels? I have found two differentiating factors.

First, time. *Lust* wants what it wants when it wants it. Love wants what the other wants and/or what is best. A seducer will not stand the test of time. He will move on if he doesn't get what he wants. I have noticed that there appears to be a "third date" social expectation to have sex. Romantic sit-coms reference this deadline as though it was first discovered carved into the boulders of Stonehenge. I think it is unwise, but then I injured my head when I fell off the ark. Time is a great test of a man's intentions.

Secondly, a man who is sincere won't do anything that might result in losing you. A man who only wants to score will take the risk of offending you just in case it works. If he criticizes you about waiting to have sex, makes fun of you, pressures you by not keeping his hands off of you, he is telling you something—and it's not that he is so crazy about you he can't help himself. He is telling you that he is not concerned about losing you.

A suitor will love you if you do and love you if you don't. A seducer won't love you if you do and will leave you if you don't. (Actually, a seducer will leave you either way.)

One man told me that for men, sex is not the beginning of something, as in, "Now we are in a relationship!" It is not the consummation of anything, as in, "Now we are a couple!" It's just sex. That isn't very pleasant to hear but it has an interesting flip side. This man fell in love with a girl who had waited to have sex until she married, and she asked him to wait until their wedding night. Here is what he said: "I love you, and I will love you if we have sex now or wait until after the wedding. It doesn't make any difference to me. If you want to wait, we'll wait."

They waited. She was happy. He was fine with it. Sex didn't make a difference; it was just sex—but in a good way! It didn't affect his love for her or his commitment to her one way or the other.

Remember that love is not trying to score. A suitor is trying to win, yes, but he is trying to win your heart.

My advice? Go slowly. Especially when he wants to go fast. Time will tell.

THE POWER OF POLITE

One day as I sat at my receptionist/secretary desk in a radio station, a young account executive strolled by with a small stack of paperwork uplifted in her right hand which she proceeded to drop from shoulder height onto my desk with a resounding smack. "I'll need these by noon," she said without looking at me, and strolled away. It felt insulting. I have never forgotten it.

A few years later, I worked for a large law firm, and the managing attorney would often walk down the row of word processors with dictation projects in hand. "Hey, kiddo!" he would cheerfully greet me, always followed by, "Could you do me a big favor?" And he'd ask me to transcribe a deposition or type up a pleading. It felt considerate. It made me feel happy to do it. I have never forgotten it.

A friend of mine who had done the hard work of being a server would always add, "when you get a sec" to any request when she was in a restaurant. "May we please have some more water when you get a sec?" So simple, yet it implied that the server had tables other than hers and was not her personal peon.

When I think of all the people with whom I transact business, I personally marvel at how impersonal I am with them sometimes. At the grocery store checkout, I pay more attention to processing my debit card than I do to the person processing my purchase. I never look at their name tag. I do at least say, "Thank you" when they give me the receipt, but those two words seem to exhaust my powers of light conversation. Why they don't drop-kick me out the door is a miracle of self-restraint. I certainly deserve it.

Because I'd prefer not to be booted out and land on the pavement with a cracked coccyx, I am going to notice names, exchange easy-going comments about the weather, say thank you, and wish them a great day, and otherwise acknowledge their value as an employee and a fellow human being from now on. I will try to soften my requests with things like, "I need your help with …" and "Do you have time to …" After all, I don't want someone to be thinking about me what I was thinking about the account executive who plopped the papers on my desk. "Why you obnoxious little twerp, you can just ***** ******* and ******* while you're at it!" Don't bother counting the asterisks to figure out the words. I just made them up. But you get the idea!

THE SOLUTION FOR PEOPLE WHO
ARE ALWAYS LATE

I was born promptly. Other than that, I was always late. To everything. To a timely person I was fingernails on chalkboard. Why couldn't I just get up fifteen minutes earlier? Set my clock back? Put out my clothes for the morning, make my lunch the night before?

The mystery was that I could do all of those things and *still* be between ten to fifteen minutes late. How was that even possible?

In desperation, I tried setting the clock back earlier and earlier. But no matter how early I set the clock, I was always the same ten to fifteen minutes late.

Then one glorious day, I found the solution. I planned to be fifteen minutes early to attend an 8:45 a.m. music rehearsal before church began at 9 a.m. and noticed I arrived exactly on time for the service!

I tried it at work. I planned to arrive fifteen minutes early and have a nice cup of coffee before sitting down at my desk. I arrived exactly on time! It was almost miraculous how precisely this technique worked!

The solution is to plan to be as early as you are usually late, and you'll be on time! I know it's a bit mind-bending, but here's how it works.

Everyone has an inner sense of time. People are usually the same amount of time early (Carol Burnett is always ten minutes early to appointments) or the same amount of time late. Both timely and late people have a sense of time that relaxes when they have plenty of time and gets nervous if they are running out of time. The difference with the always-late person is that their sense of time is a certain number of minutes off. If you adjust for those minutes (by planning to be early) it will function to get you there on time.

It is curious that it doesn't work to just set the clock back, because somehow your inner clock "knows" you have done this and simply factors in this extra time and you still end up late. Only planning to be early by the same amount of time you are usually late will cause your faulty clock to get you there on time!

This is a great solution for Human Resource departments to share with employees who are imperiling their employment by clocking in late. And it's wonderful to share with students who always miss part of their classes.

One woman was always ten minutes late to her adult education class. She protested that she had a child to get up and get ready, and there was just no way she could be at class at 8 a.m. like everyone else. The earliest she could get there was 8:10 a.m. So, the professor agreed, "For you, ten minutes late will be considered on time." Guess what time the woman showed up for class the next day? 8:20 a.m. Now you know the reason why.

THOSE (NOT REALLY) LYING
BASTARDS

The true skill of advertising is to get you to think an ad said something it didn't actually say so you will buy something it made you think you wanted.

If you had to read that two times, I'm not surprised.

Like you, I have spent a lifetime buying products. There is no material thing in my home that I didn't buy. I don't think of myself as gullible. I am a reasonable consumer who buys what I need or sometimes merely want, and I can make decisions between the variety of products that are available through different brands.

Or can I? The advice in this chapter will come in the form of ways to read and view advertising so you can tell how it is emotionally prompting you, how it is leading you to believe its claims, and how it is, basically, getting you to think you need their product, make you want it, and make you buy it.

All is fair in love, war, and sales. This is a brief self-defense chapter.

My first advice is to watch for "qualifiers." They are rampant in beauty products. Let's say I am selling you a moisturizer, and I say it "helps to reduce the appearance of wrinkles." Somehow the message that sticks is "wrinkles." Do you think it makes wrinkles go away? Be smaller? Be not so deep? Here is the magic I worked that you might not have noticed:

I didn't say anything about wrinkles at all. Read it again. I only spoke of their appearance.

This spares the product manufacturer in a court of law if you sue because the cream doesn't change your wrinkles. They never said it would. "Helps to" and "reduces" are purposely vague and almost impossible to measure. "Appearance" is so subjective as to be almost meaningless. The selling maneuver is the impression these qualifiers give. *Qualifiers cause us to assume what has not been said.* Not that I'm saying that any ad I have ever read has seeded their copy with qualifiers in order to allow its readers to arrive at erroneous conclusions that cause them to buy the product. Surely not.

"Dermatologist tested" and "dermatologist recommended" have very different meanings, but both contain the medical word, "dermatologist." Some may think it implies that the product may be science-based, perhaps even science-verified. Others may consider it safer or even medically approved because doctors are involved. Like the white lab coat, the word "dermatologist" can inspire trust.

Then there are ads that tell you nothing and let you tell yourself everything. They do it with suggestive copy or emotionally evocative images. Research the original Lady Clairol® ads if you want to see how it's done. Those ads are genius. Did they work? Phenomenally well. Their effect is still reverberating today! At work, I noticed that there were very few women who did not have some sort of highlights in their hair.

"Is it true blondes have more fun?" sings the happy chorus in the ad. "A Lady Clairol blonde, a silky shining blonde!" Then a mellow male voice tempts, "Why not be a blonde and see?" Note that the questions make you curious and perhaps a little uncertain of your not-blonde beauty. Silky and shining are such youthful, wonderful words! Suddenly nothing seems so shiny as blonde hair reflecting sunlight! In ecstatic tones, a female voice exclaims, "If I have one life to live, let me live it as a blonde!" The decision is so thrilling you may forget it isn't your own!

The ad's visuals include a carefree life lived on a tennis court (an expensive sport many may not even play, but it is glamorously aspirational, so who cares?), at the pool, and on an elegant evening of dancing. You may infer from these that if your hair were blonde you would instantly transport into the upper class. The thought that you could be blonde and not get any closer to glamour than the local bowling alley doesn't occur. We want to believe in dreams and escape reality, and advertisements are swift to help us believe we can—if only we buy their product.

The musical chant, "A Lady Clairol blonde, a silky shining blonde!" is repeated so often it becomes a beauty manifesto. We don't even think to ask, "So what are brunettes? Ratty and dull?" And of course, the Lady Clairol blonde in the ads may be skimming along on a bike and cavorting with handsome men. One ad ends in a marriage ceremony! If you just changed your hair color, all this endless, iridescent joy would be yours as all the dull, boring brunettes sulk on the sidelines. Not that the ad actually said that. But when you see it so clearly, how can you not think it?

The only claim the ad actually made was "silky, shiny," which describes most hair after a shampoo! The rest was concocted of images and a question *they never answered* that was designed to tap into any insecurity about beauty, popularity, and youth: "Is it true blondes have more fun?" Why did light hair seem more glamorous in an age that fairly pulsated with the simmering sexuality of Ava Gardner, Sophia Loren, and Elizabeth Taylor? The ads didn't say. And viewers were so enthralled they didn't think of it.

Advertising preys on our insecurities and panders to our aspirations. Yet in a way, it isn't to blame if it misleads us because it is only leading us where we want to go. Their product may be the way, but we choose the destination.

What are they trying to make you think? What is the implied promise? What do you want to do or be that the ad wants to cash in on?

"UltraBrite® gives your mouth sex appeal!" The sheer genius of this highly successful ad is what you may think it said. Think fast! Did it just say UltraBrite gives you sex appeal? Many people say yes. They are wrong. It specifically said only your *mouth* will have sex appeal, and they clearly defined sex appeal as clean freshness (which any toothpaste will provide). The rest of you will remain as is! The product flew off the shelves because anything that promises to impart sex appeal is something most of us want to buy. The fact that they restricted it to our mouth and defined it as clean freshness escaped our attention because we were too busy grabbing our car keys to drive to the store and buy it.

Some ads hardly say anything but imply a great deal. A classic ad for Johnny Walker™ Black Label™ scotch pictures two elegant mansions set back on a swath of green lawn against a twilight sky, with one neighbor at the other's door asking, "I was wondering if I could possibly borrow a cup of Johnnie Walker Black Label." The implication? It is in every wealthy home as a matter of course. Common folk may borrow a cup of milk, but rich people will go next door knowing more Johnnie Walker Black Label scotch will be there. But the magnificent inference is that by buying a bottle of this product, it will somehow make you like one of these wealthy, sophisticated people! It's the only part of their life you can afford but it gives you admittance to the whole dream. True, you don't have the mansion or the income that supports it, but by heaven you can have a bottle of Johnnie Walker Black Label! Can you think of another ad like that? I can.

Two limos pull up side by side, two car windows roll silently down, one elegant person asks, "Pardon me, but do you have any Grey Poupon®?" and the reply is purred, "But of course." Notice that they don't even mention what it is—mustard! There are many Dijon mustards, but I would be willing to bet very few have the name recognition or elegant reputation of Grey Poupon. And again, in buying this product and holding a bottle of Grey Poupon in your hand, you may not have the Rolls Royce but by heaven, you have the mustard!

I always have a bottle of Grey Poupon in my refrigerator. I am a natural blonde, but I would have tried going blonde based on those Lady Clairol ads if I hadn't been one naturally. My moisturizer is dermatologist tested. I wholeheartedly believe every promise every perfume ad has ever made. It seems even an advertising copywriter can fall for ads.

WAITING ROOM

Waiting room. Isn't that the place where magazines go to age away? This is another kind. It means you wait to speak, thereby giving people room to think and speak further. You give them *waiting room.*

Conversations

The best interviewing technique I've found is not talking. It applies to everyday conversations as well. Here's how it works.

You ask a question, and they answer. According to the rhythm of a conversation, this is when you would speak again. Try waiting instead. In that pause, they are thinking. Considering. Remembering. It is so hard to allow three seconds of silence, yet if you do, you will hear something deeper, more intriguing, more informative than the first part of their answer. It can become the best part of the conversation. In the context of an interview, their extended reply can cause the whole interview to pivot and go in a new direction more interesting than the one you had planned with your list of questions.

I discovered this technique during a phone interview when I paused to find my place in my questions list.

The subject continued to talk, and soon a jewel of a quote was sparkling on the page! Their enthusiasm brightened, and their words began to flow.

When I talk with friends, I tend to comment, offer advice (I'm writing a book of it, for Pete's sake), and in general try to support and help them. Why I never think of just shutting up, I'll never know. Whenever I let the conversational focus remain on my friend, I am always touched by what they share. And I notice that if I can just glue my lips to the coffee cup and keep sipping, they will arrive at conclusions and insights that help them more than anything I could have said.

Listening is the greatest thing you can say.

Meetings

In meetings, everyone has something to say. It is filling their minds while they dutifully fake focusing their attention on what the others are contributing. Although it's difficult to refrain from shooting your hand in the air like a kid in a classroom when you have something of value to contribute, something important and possibly groundbreaking—wait. If you let everyone else speak first, they will be able to hear you when you speak last. Also, people tend to remember the first and the last of things. The middle is a bit hazy. Speak first and risk not being heard at all. Speak last and be heard and remembered.

Another reason to wait until others have spoken is that even though what you have to say is the growth concept of the century and most certainly a brilliant financial unicorn of an idea with money-making magic in its veins, it could be profoundly impacted by new information that will emerge as the others contribute around the conference table. When you listen to everyone else before you speak, you can adapt your contribution accordingly.

But what if someone else comes up with your idea first? That was always my fear but never the case in the entire length of my career. However, it was often the case that I spoke too soon, and the impact was diluted. Wait.

WHEN A BEST FRIEND ISN'T ANYMORE

This is a chapter that is hard to write, not because I don't have experience with the subject, but because I do.

Somewhere inside me, alive and well, are a little kid and a teenager. It gets crowded in there. They remember the schools I went to, the friends, and a bewildering kaleidoscope of experiences. I didn't find life a very pleasant thing to live when I was young, and I remember those who made it survivable.

Lina and I were lifelong friends because our parents double-dated long before our respective ova drifted down our mothers' fallopian tubes. She was a true, fierce friend, and no one could make me laugh more than Lina. My friend Claudia was a sultry beauty with a wacky sense of humor that made life worth living. We met in third grade. One of her high school boyfriends had a best friend who became my first boyfriend, first kiss, and first proposal. You don't forget things like that.

My friends were successful at life, and they saved mine. My loyalty to them is written as a postscript on the Ten Commandment tablets. So just imagine whacking a mule across the forehead with a two-by-four to get his attention and seeing his eyes cross and his floppy ears droop in dismay, and you'll have me when one of them changed beyond recognition and became hostile, and another simply became busy and stayed that way.

Lina disappeared into a form of religion that thought of all things as positives. The worst that life could bring was joyfully celebrated as the best thing that could have happened. There was no pause to process the pain. The switch flipped to the happy dance. I understood the precept but found that I couldn't honestly tell her how I thought or felt anymore. She wanted to guard her spirit. Although she was positive, her sense of humor disappeared and her defensiveness against any perceived negativity manifested as anger. My sunny, funny Lina had been subsumed, and I couldn't do anything about it. She was gone. And there is no one so gone as someone who is still there but is not the same person.

Has Claudia changed? Not a bit. Life with four grown daughters and Parkinson's has not dimmed her earthy sense of humor or her precious ability to sympathize and give brief, wise comments that lighten both heavy loads and darkness. But she is busy, involved in the complexities and crises of family life, as indeed she should be. The relationship must be maintained within the parameters of a few Facebook messages once in a while and perhaps a rare phone call when she can schedule one. We will always love each other. I miss her more than I can say.

I know of several times when I didn't particularly want to maintain a friendship, and there honestly wasn't any definable reason other than the friendship was perfect in its time, but that time was in the past. I feel awful about it, but there isn't much I can do about it either! This self-knowledge, most unfortunately, doesn't help me give advice on this subject. Why do I still love Claudia, miss a Lina who no longer exists, but am fine with not seeing Betty Sue anymore? I don't know!

Have we really come down to "you can't help who you love?" I think we may have. All I can do is apply my emotions in a relationship I have allowed to lapse as a balm to the wound of a relationship that has lapsed when I am the one who still cares. The friends I am "over" did nothing wrong. The friends who are "over" me have turned a page in their lives. My page-turning is a little behind the times, that's all. I want them to go back and be the same, just as others want me to go back and be the same. That won't happen because it can't happen. No one can go back. Friendships that last don't "go back"—they continue from the past through to the present.

My advice here cannot be my own; it must come from someone wiser than I am. "To everything there is a season, and a time to every purpose under heaven." Ecclesiastes 3:1. Today is always the season to find present-time friends.

THE YELLOW BRICK ROAD

"College is the gateway to a great career and a successful life," they say. "First college, then career. That's the yellow brick road!" I'm not altogether sure that is true. A lot of great things have emerged from garages instead of colleges, and I'm not talking about cars. Chilly garages where a one-hundred-watt bulb labors to light up the dusty dimness have turned out to be the humble wombs of worldwide success for some people.

Think musicians! The longhaired lay-abouts sit there and plink and plunk away the hours they could be studying for high school botany so they can go to college and get an entry level job and sit through eight million meetings as they snail-crawl their way to management and bluff their way through eight million more meetings until they retire and can finally take up a hobby in their garage—like learning to play the guitar.

Think software gurus! Geeky software guys hang out in anonymous garages hidden away from jaunty jocks and unattainable beauties (who will try and marry them for their money someday), creating technology that will reinvent life as we know it and force their high school alumni to continually attend webinars to keep up with the pace as the latest software programs outdate their resumes and their work vocabulary every six months, embarrassing them in meetings until retirement alone can stop the tech-shaming. The geeky software guys, however, retire fairly young, rich and on the cover of every magazine except Sports Illustrated.

It really doesn't matter if it's the "road less travelled by" or the mainstream highway of life as long as the road you take is authentically your road.

What about regrets? Regrets are chances not taken, opportunities passed up, and obstacles allowed to look larger than they actually are (think side-view car mirrors). Regrets are taking someone else's advice or listening to someone else's voice instead of your own. Regret is realizing you ignored yourself, over-ruled yourself, and now you are someone other than who you would have been. You are other-created. That is regret.

Let's say you want to trot around the globe without a root to your name and experience all the wonders of the world. Others prefer you pursue a career in law because someone will always be suing someone, and if that isn't job security, what is? And it's so much nicer than being a mortician, adds your Aunt Edna. After all, others inquire, when it comes time to retire from your wanderings, what are you going to do? Sit on an ice floe and wait for a polar bear? If global warning persists, even that option will disappear! Whereas after a career of bellowing, "I object" at disrupting intervals, you can retire and cruise away on a yacht named "I Rest My Case."

But what if all those years of practicing law are formaldehyde to your spirit? The sadness of the unsung song of your soul will not be mitigated by a financially pleasant coda. On the other hand (we need more hands at times like these, don't we?), if you spend your life as a blithe Peter Pan flying from one adventure to the next, you may perhaps *not* despair that you deprived yourself of a life you didn't desire in the first place! And even if at the end all you have is the ability to say, "Where is the bathroom" in twenty-seven different languages, you will feel the peace of a fulfilled life.

Now what if your family is Woodstockian in nature if not in experience, and there you are, an incomprehensible little misfit, longing for Torts and gearing up for legal battle like an Olympian, and your family can't understand where they went wrong. Reverse and apply all the above thoughts.

Your dad is a doctor, and you want to be a mechanic. Your dad is a mechanic, and you want to be a doctor. Your mom stayed at home and wants the same for you. Your mom stayed at home and doesn't want the same for you. Your brother is a doctor. Your sister is an attorney. You are fascinated with earthworms. Where the heck did you come from? Doesn't matter. What matters is where you want to go, which is based on who you are and who you want to be and what you want to do.

The point is only and always who YOU are now and who you want to be. We may all flow into the same sea but we are different rivers and we must "go with our own flow," so to speak.

Follow your own yellow brick road.

ACKNOWLEDGEMENTS

Cheryl McCollum

When my friend said I should write a book, I asked her, 'About what?' She said she didn't know. She only knew that she saved my emails through the years because they gave her counsel and comfort, and it was a pleasure to re-read them. It was a wonderful thing for her to say and I experienced a feeling of surprise and happiness—a feeling I think we call "joy." I also felt floor-flat humble that someone so deeply intelligent as Cheryl would say such a thing of my thoughts. But I had to tell her, "I don't have a book in me," because I didn't. And then (drum roll, please) the word "advice" appeared in my mind as clearly as if it were written on a wall. It was the only official 'vision' I've ever had. And this book began.

I sat down at my laptop and proceeded to write 43 chapters of advice in two months. The first was "Yellow Brick Road." Each morning felt like Christmas morning because I woke up early with excitement and sat down with anticipation (and coffee) to write.

Cheryl's involvement did not end with her suggestion. I sent her every chapter and she critiqued them all. She's a natural editor, affirming specifically and course-correcting gently with equal skill. This book would not have happened without her. It wouldn't even have occurred to me.

Deborah Jefferies

Cheryl said one of her neighbors was an excellent graphic designer in high demand. Would I mind if Cheryl shared a few chapters with Deborah in case she wanted to design the book cover? The chapters were sent, and this incredibly talented artist said she loved them and believed in the value of the book so much that yes, she would re-arrange her 2021 project schedule to include the cover. It was like Steven Spielberg saying he'd love to direct my film.

Pauline Harris

Pauline is a prolific writer and a veteran in the publishing industry. Her knowledge is encyclopedic and her patience apparently inexhaustible. As a newbie to it all, I needed the publishing equivalent of a Sherpa, particularly one who would talk slowly and clearly when explaining how to cooperate with the "algorithm" (the what?) in online marketing and promotion. Would you like that for your book? Wish granted. Go to www.paulineharriseditorial.com.

AUTHOR BIO

Teresa Pesce lives in the beauty of Idaho in a postcard-perfect town of wonderful people. As a playwright she loves to work with actors and direct her plays on the stage of the historic Panida Theater. Shaded by chestnut trees, she enjoys home life with her husband Jimmy, a tabby cat named Tabbycat and a dog named Dog. And a dog named Napoo—named by the grandchildren who are obviously better at coming up with names.

Made in the USA
Las Vegas, NV
05 August 2022

52753651R00100